WA
METH

Fifteen Count
Buckinghamshire and Hertfordshire

C000076115

Countryside Books' walking guides cover most areas of England and Wales and include the following series:

County Rambles
Walks For Motorists
Exploring Long Distance Paths
Literary Walks

A complete list is available from the publishers:

3 Catherine Road, Newbury, Berkshire

WALKS IN METROLAND

Fifteen Country Rambles
around Buckinghamshire
and Hertfordshire

Liz Roberts

With Historical Notes

COUNTRYSIDE BOOKS
NEWBURY, BERKSHIRE

First Published 1991
© Liz Roberts 1991

All rights reserved
No reproduction permitted without
the prior permission of the publishers:

COUNTRYSIDE BOOKS
3 Catherine Road
Newbury, Berkshire

ISBN 1 85306 121 2

Cover photograph of Coombe Hill
taken by John Bethell
Sketch maps by Bernard Roberts

Produced through MRM Associates Ltd., Reading
Printed in England by J.W. Arrowsmith Ltd., Bristol

Metroland

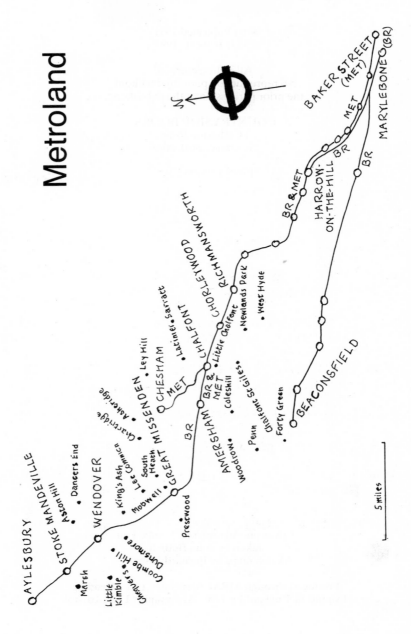

Contents

Introduction

'I know a land where the wild flowers grow,
Near, near at hand if by train you go,
'Metroland', 'Metroland',
Meadows sweet have a golden glow,
Hills are green as the vales below
In 'Metroland', 'Metroland'.

'Metroland', 'Metroland',
Leafy dell and woodland fair,
Land of love and hope and peace;
Land where all your troubles cease–
'Metroland', 'Metroland',
Waft, oh, waft me there;
Hearts are lighter, eyes are brighter
In 'Metroland', 'Metroland'.

Thus wrote Private George Sims longingly from the filth and degradation of trench warfare in the First World War.

'Metroland' was really just an advertising gimmick in a campaign by the old Metropolitan Railway Company to use its surplus land for the development of housing estates near its extension from Baker Street out through Middlesex, Hertfordshire and Buckinghamshire to Aylesbury and thence to the Midlands. Railway advertisements in the 1920s and 1930s conjured up visions of a suburban paradise in green fields and woodlands, with quiet avenues of small, affordable houses, indoor sanitation and a 'sunburst' of coloured glass in the front door. Each would have a sunny garden where the children could play in clean, fresh air and flowers could be grown among the gnomes and ornamental ponds.

For the rambler today, 'Metroland is a country with elastic boundaries which each visitor can draw for himself, as Stevenson drew his map of Treasure Island. As much of the countryside as you can comfortably cover on foot from one Metropolitan railway station to another you may add to your private and individual map of Metroland. It is a country of hills and valleys, ridges and hollows. Go where you will the landscape is well farmed; the eye ranges from wood to wood, from tower to steeple, whin-clad common and fields which still laugh with golden corn.' So the 1920s advertisement ran, and the same is true today.

It is difficult now to realise that at that time Willesden Green, Neasden, Ickenham and Ruislip were tiny hamlets set on three sides of a village green, with a pond in the middle and the church occupying the fourth side. Difficult, too, to envisage Rickmansworth and Uxbridge as 'small market towns' but this was so until the Met began its developments in 1919, inspired by the forceful Sir Edward Watkin, with his vision of a main line railway which would link the Midlands to the Channel ports. Sadly, development of the line beyond Aylesbury has ceased and the station at Quainton Road is now used as a railway museum.

These 15 walks have been chosen to take the walker back in time to join the cheerful groups who, between the wars, came out from London on the Met each weekend to walk, perhaps, through the lovely valley of the river Chess or over wide fields and through the magnificent, timeless beechwoods, or among the tiny hamlets and villages on the chalky uplands of the Chiltern hills.

Not all the walks are round walks but all start and finish at a station. The train journey from Marylebone, once past Harrow, is a delight in itself, plunging at once into peaceful countryside; the intricate pattern of lakes and waterways near Rickmansworth, gently sloping hills around Chorleywood and then the steeply wooded slopes and farmland, typical of the Chiltern landscape. Facilities for car parking have been noted with each walk for those who prefer their own wheels.

From Baker Street, Metropolitan Line trains run half-hourly 7 days per week to Rickmansworth, Chorleywood, Chalfont & Latimer, and Amersham. Change at Chalfont & Latimer for Chesham.

From Marylebone, BR trains run half-hourly from Monday to Saturday continuing past Amersham to Great Missenden, Wendover, Stoke Mandeville and Aylesbury. On Sundays it is necessary to travel by Metropolitan Line from Baker Street to Amersham and an *hourly* BR shuttle service operates between Amersham and Aylesbury to take passengers on or back.

INTRODUCTION

For Beaconsfield, use the BR High Wycombe/Banbury line from Marylebone which operates 7 days per week. The trains are more sporadic; half-hourly early and late and hourly only in the middle of the day. It is wise to check on all train times before starting off.

Wherever possible the names of good pubs and cafes on the route have been mentioned and the short, historical notes at the end of each walk provide some information on what to look out for on the various routes. There is an abundance of wild life to be observed, plenty of wild flowers in their seasons and it goes without saying that the scenery is spectacular and varied.

The sketch map that accompanies each walk is designed to guide walkers to the starting point and give a simple yet accurate idea of the route to be taken. For those who like the benefit of detailed maps the relevant Ordnance Survey 1:50,000 Landranger series will be useful. Please remember the Country Code and make sure gates are not left open or any farm animals disturbed.

No special equipment is needed to enjoy the countryside on foot, but do wear a stout pair of shoes and remember that at least one muddy patch is likely even on the sunniest day.

Many hours of enjoyment have gone into preparing these walks. I hope the reader will go out and enjoy them too.

Liz Roberts
March 1991

Rickmansworth, West Hyde and Newland Park

Introduction: This is a varied walk, mostly on level ground, but there is some steepish up and down work. The route leads for ½ mile or so through the suburbs of Rickmansworth from the station and, quite suddenly, there is open country; beautiful lakes, the dreamy Grand Union Canal, wide fields and woodlands to walk.

Distance: 8½ to 9 miles. Allow a good 4 hours for walking, stopping to watch the wildlife, to admire the scenery and take refreshment. This is a walk with many different things to enjoy. OS Landranger Map Sheet 176 West London.

Refreshments: There are pubs galore in Rickmansworth; about ⅓ of the way round the walk is the *Fisheries Inn* at West Hyde and, further on, the *Dumbbell Inn*. Both serve hot and cold lunches.

How to get there: By train from Marylebone or Baker Street; please read the Introduction to the book for more information. By road on the M25, leaving it at Exit 17 for Rickmansworth and Watford. The car park is close to the station (both are signposted) and is free to users at weekends but there is a charge for the day during the week. GR: 945/057

The walk: Turn right out of the station and right again under a railway bridge. At the T-junction at the far end turn right into High Street and then left at the Western Inn into Wensum Way. Follow this to the Ebury roundabout, cross to the A412 (Old Uxbridge Rd) and follow this road into Mill End. Very soon take a marked footpath on the left opposite Coleman's Tyre Centre. This

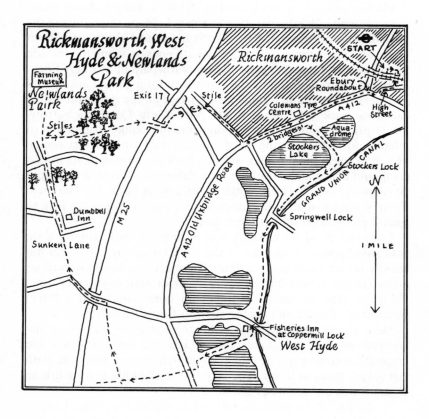

is a very new footpath and does not appear on the Ordnance Survey Map; it is shown on the map which goes with these directions. Follow the path over a wooden bridge, left on the other side and then right over a new metal bridge. Heron live among the reeds separating these narrow waterways.

Having crossed the bridge follow the path straight ahead across a narrow spit of land separating Stockers Lake on the right and the Aquadrome on the left. The lake is home to Canada and Brent geese and many types of duck. The path goes on along the far side of the lake and emerges onto the canal towpath at Stockers Lock. Turn right here and follow the canal path for a good 2 miles, with Stockers Lake behind a small mixed wood on the right and rolling farmland backed by wooded hills on the left. Colourful narrow-boats ply the water or lie moored on the banks, fishermen sit silently for hours gazing at stationary rods with an occasional twitch to rouse them from reverie, a flock of geese inhabits the far bank and ducks and moorhens hurry about the water. Just before Springwell Lock is a large pottery on the right bank, the Harefield Pottery, and a small lane crosses a bridge from it over the lock to gravel pits hidden on the other bank.

Continue along the towpath past Springwell Lock, coming soon into woodland on both sides of the canal; some majestic trees but mostly rather small and scrubby. There are patches of waterlilies whose bright yellow flowers are a cheerful sight in summer time. Walk on past the pretty cottages on both banks and a large, apparently disused mill on the right to Copper Mill Lock.

Here go up onto the road at the *Fisheries Inn* and on to the footpath on the left signposted Old Uxbridge Road. Cross a stile opposite and over a lane and then straight ahead along the path between 2 strips of water. The lake on the right has private fishing rights which are zealously guarded!

At the end of the path turn left and then right over Shire Lane to a main road. Cross with care onto a broad track opposite and follow it for about ¾ mile to a cross-track. Turn right alongside the field to walk up and downhill. There are beautiful views of the countryside here on the right; the narrow tree-filled valley through which the canal runs is clearly visible and wooded hills clamber beyond it. On the left the 20th century intrudes noisily as the path runs almost parallel with the M25 across a field. At the top of the path turn left onto a lane which crosses the motorway and meanders gently downhill between thick old hedges. After about 300 yards, on a bend, take the marked path on the right and follow this ancient, flinty sunken lane for about ½ mile to a lane. Bear left and follow the lane straight ahead past the *Dumbbell Inn* and 2 pretty cottages on the right, ignoring all footpath signs. After a mile the lane is shaded by woods on both sides and a crossroad opposite the entrance to Newlands Park, with its farming museum, is reached. Cross the road to take the bridleway to the right of the College entrance and after about 200 yards take a marked path over a stile on the right.

There are 2 more stiles to cross, well hidden in the hedge on the left and, about halfway down, a third stile which brings the walker into Bottom Wood. As far as possible follow a fairly well-defined footpath straight down through the wood; there are various diversions round fallen trees. Emerging from the far end of the wood, over or between 2 metal poles, go diagonally across the field making toward the motorway which you will hear, and soon see, as you breast the hill. At the far right corner of the field is a stile onto a bridge crossing the motorway. On the far side take a metalled track which runs downhill almost parallel with the road. Keep to this track, ignoring a turning on the right, and follow it as it bears right and then left under a road bridge. Go across the field on the other side of the bridge and, at a stile, turn right into a lane. Follow the lane for about ¾ mile to return to the A412 and turn left.

Now there is a walk of about 1 mile through Mill End and the suburbs of Rickmansworth; not very inspiring but the rest of the walk makes up for it. Cross the road at the pedestrian lights by the small arcade of shops. You can buy ice-cold drinks from the little supermarket before crossing. Soon the Ebury roundabout appears, cross into Wensum Way and turn right into the High Street. Take the first turning on the left and walk under the railway bridge to find the station on the left at the top. The car park is just to the right of this little road's exit at the station.

Historical notes

Rickmansworth: The rivers Colne, Gade and Chess all converge near Rickmansworth so it is not surprising that there is plenty of water to see there. It was once a flourishing market town but is now mostly a residential district.

The High Street has a number of excellent examples of the Georgian period, notably Basing House, which was once the home of William Penn, the founder of Pennsylvania.

Newland Park College lies just off the main route and in its grounds is the Chiltern Open Air Museum. Volunteers have spent much time and enthusiastic energy reconstructing farm-buildings and dwellings, from an Iron Age house and a Saxon bakehouse to a 19th century vicarage 'room'. Almost every weekend there are displays and events depicting a period of history centred around one of the buildings. Even when there is no display in progress, the museum is well worth a visit. It is open from 1st April to the end of October on Wednesdays and Sundays from 2pm to 6pm, and from July to September it is open on all days except Monday and Tuesday, at the same time.

If you want to visit this fascinating piece of 'history' continue on the bridleway ahead from the back entrance to Newland Park College and the museum is reached in a short ¼ mile. Return down the bridleway to rejoin the route of the original walk.

The Grand Union Canal starts in East London and ends in the Midlands and it, and the various 'arms' joining it, formed a busy waterway for the transport of goods to and from the industrial Midlands to the commercial capital. Now it is virtually disused as a method of transport other than for pleasure but the colourful narrowboats still judder along, no longer pulled by horses on the towpath but motorised for holiday-makers. Some are moored to provide homes.

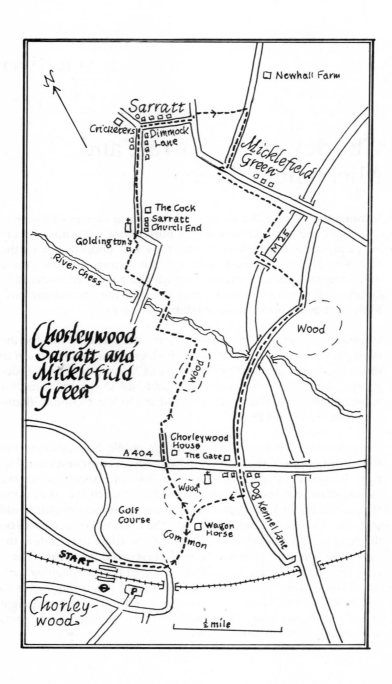

Chorleywood, Sarratt and Micklefield Green

Introduction: This quite short walk takes in a variety of country-side from the turfy common at Chorleywood, downhill to the peaceful banks of the tiny river Chess and uphill again to the charming village of Sarratt with its 12th century church. Along quiet country lanes, it returns through the hamlet of Micklefield Green and across wide fields, crossing over the terrifyingly busy M25 motorway; ancient and modern side by side.

Distance: 6½ miles. There are 2 short, steep climbs but for the most part the walk is on fairly level high ground. The exception to this is the lovely little valley of the river Chess traversed for about a mile. Allow 3 hours for the walk and add to this any time for refreshment. OS Landranger Map Sheet 176 West London. Path-finder Sheet TQ 09/19.

Refreshments: There are a number of public houses along the route; just opposite the start of the walk, across the common to the right from the car park or station, is the *Old Shepherd*. In the middle of the common, alongside a tiny lane which bisects it, is the *Wagon Horse*, tucked into the corner by some delightful old cottages. There are 2 pubs in Sarratt; the *Cock* lies on the route on the right just past the church and just off the route to the left at the top of the lane is the *Cricketers*; both serve good bar meals. There is an inviting notice on the wall at the top of the lane leading back into Chorleywood which just says TEAS but it was impossible to discover where they were! The *Gate* is about 100 yards to the right at the top of this lane. There are plenty of excellent picnic spots with lovely views to admire while eating.

17

How to get there: By train from Marylebone or Baker Street; please read the Introduction to the book for further train information. By road on the M25 leaving it at Exit 18 for Chorleywood and then taking the A404 for Amersham. In just under 2 miles turn left at a signpost for Chorleywood Station. Follow the road past some houses and immediately before a railway bridge turn sharply left into Station Approach. Go past the station following signs for the car park and turning sharply right over another railway bridge to find the car park at the end of a little right turn after a few yards. There is space here and there is a charge per day. Alternatively, the car can be parked on a small gravelly square on the left immediately before the right turn over the railway bridge; parking here is free but the space soon goes. From the Amersham direction, go along the A404 for Watford and the Chorleywood Station turn is on the right exactly 2 miles from the Little Chalfont roundabout. GR: 025/961

The walk: Turn right out of the station and walk along the lane towards the car park as far as the railway bridge. From the car park turn right and retrace the route back over the railway bridge. At the bridge take the well-trodden footpath on the right straight across the common. At a fork in the path by some pretty cottages and the *Wagon Horse*, bear left and then turn left onto a grassy 'ride' alongside a tiny new beech tree next to a 'Horse Track' sign, to walk up through a little thicket of birch and cherry trees. Turn right onto the golf course at the end of the wood and walk alongside it, past a putting green and into another little thicket. Go straight ahead on the far side across the cricket field with the cricket clubhouse on the left and the church on the right.

Reaching the A404, cross it near Chorleywood House, a large white building, and take the marked footpath 30 yards to the left of the house and opposite the clubhouse. The path starts as a metalled road, which follow ahead for about ¼ mile till it ends with a metal gate opposite on a cross track. Here turn right and then bear left downhill on a steep, flinty path between tall chestnut and beech trees making for the Chess valley. Here are fine views of gently undulating landscape all around and the holly bushes along the path are bright with scarlet berries in the autumn.

Cross the stile at the end of the path and turn left to follow a path between hedges, go over a stile and cross the river by a little footbridge on the right. The river is shallow and pebbly-bottomed, the water clear and fast-flowing and trusses of watercress grow along its edges. From here there are wide, sweeping views of farmland beyond the valley. Turn left at the gate to carry on alongside the river and over a little lane to the path opposite. Just before a group of cottages, turn right to go over a stile to follow the path against the fence on the left. The large, cream-painted house on the hilltop is Goldington's. Pause at the top of the hill to look back over the huge vista of river valley and wood-fringed fields.

Take the stile on the left at the top of the field and cross Goldington's drive to a path opposite, coming onto a lane opposite Sarratt church, with some beautiful old timbered barns to the left and charming old almshouses in a row on the right. Turn right and follow the lane past the church and the *Cock* on the right into Sarratt village, ignoring all side turnings. Opposite the village green at the top of the lane turn left to visit the *Cricketers*, otherwise cross the green to Dimmocks Lane on the right and follow it to a T-junction. Here turn left and cross the road to go over a stile opposite on the right and follow a path alongside telegraph poles across a big cultivated field. Turn right onto the farm track from Newhall Farm on the far side of the field and follow it, bearing right and left round the farm buildings, onto a lane at the little hamlet of Micklefield Green.

Turn right onto the lane and then left at the entrance to Scrubb's Farm to walk down the field alongside the hedge on the left and parallel with the lane. The M25 can be seen, and heard, at the end of the field. About 25 yards from it, turn right onto a marked path across the field now parallel with the motorway, to a stile in the far left corner. Cross the M25 by a footbridge; the spire of Chorleywood church can be seen on the hill to the right. Follow the path ahead to another lane and turn right to follow this downhill, recrossing the motorway and uphill again past tree-bordered gardens to Chorleywood, where the *Gate* is to be found about 100 yards on the right on the main A404 road.

Cross the road by the pedestrian crossing conveniently placed a few yards to the left and enter Dog Kennel Lane opposite. After about 20 yards turn right onto the common and follow the footpath straight ahead. After 200 yards turn left onto a track and follow it round the edge of the golf course, turning left again just before a group of 4 thorn trees. Go through the little thicket and turn right onto a broad path; on the left is the little group of cottages and *The Wagon Horse* in the hollow below them. Go past the cottages and take the left fork to follow the original route across the common back to the station or car park.

Historical notes

Chorleywood is a pleasant Metroland suburb situated on a high Chiltern ridge above the Chess valley. Its acres of common and its golf course were a sufficient inducement to its early settlers in the 1920s. Its church is unremarkable; a late 19th century construction by Street of flint with a tall shingle tower. C.F.A. Voysey, the architect, designed and built 2 houses here; The Orchards, in which he himself lived, and Sunnybank alongside it.

Sarratt: the Saxon church of the Holy Cross lies outside the village in a perfect rural setting and opposite it is a row of 17th century almshouses, one of which now serves as a post office. There is sinister meaning to the fact that 1 doorway in the *Cock* inn is much wider than average at 3 ft 3 inches. The reason for this is that the inn was used as a mortuary during the Plague of 1665. The back door was once the front door and had to be wide enough to admit a coffin. The plague victims were buried in a field nearby and to this day, the landlord asserts, his horses are nervous of this field and this door!

Sarratt village, with its wide green and 3 ponds, was probably once a stopping-place for drovers on their way to London with geese, sheep and other livestock. While their charges rested and drank from the ponds, the drovers themselves could find refreshment at one of the 5 inns which used to surround the green, the oldest of which was called the *Boot*.

At Sarratt Bottom, deep in the Chess valley, there were, at one time, both a flourishing mill and commercial watercress beds. Clumps of watercress still grow alongside the river.

Chesham, Chartridge and Asheridge

Introduction: Imagine the town of Chesham sitting in the palm of a slightly cupped hand and ridges of hills spreading out from it like extended fingers separated by deep dry valleys and you will have some idea of the delights this walk offers. There is a gentle climb out of Chesham through Lowndes Park, downhill into a valley and then a quite steep climb up a lane to Pednor – a grand Tudor manor and a farm. Down again into a deep valley at Pednor Bottom and steeply uphill to Chartridge. The path then winds more gently down and uphill to the next ridge, Asheridge, and then gently downhill all the way back to Chesham. The scenery is varied; wide views of rolling tree-fringed farmland, gently undulating ploughed or cultivated fields and splendid beechwoods. Wildlife abounds on the peaceful uplands; rabbits, squirrels, weasels and hosts of pheasants (with the occasional sparrow-hawk thrown in for good measure) are all at home in the fields and hedges. Along the narrow lanes only rarely is a vehicle encountered and then it is more likely to be a tractor than a car.

Distance: 7 miles – allow 3½ to 4 hours especially if refreshment at one of the pubs suitably situated on the route is envisaged. Take it gently and have time to enjoy the splendid scenery. OS Landranger Map Sheet 165 Aylesbury & Leighton Buzzard. Pathfinder Sheet SP 80/90.

Refreshments: There are no pubs in the centre of Chesham; the Broadway is now a pedestrian precinct and paved in red brick. At the junction of the main ring road and the road to Great Missenden is the tiny *White Owl Cafe* which serves tea and coffee. These can also be had at the Elgiva Hall which is passed on the way back

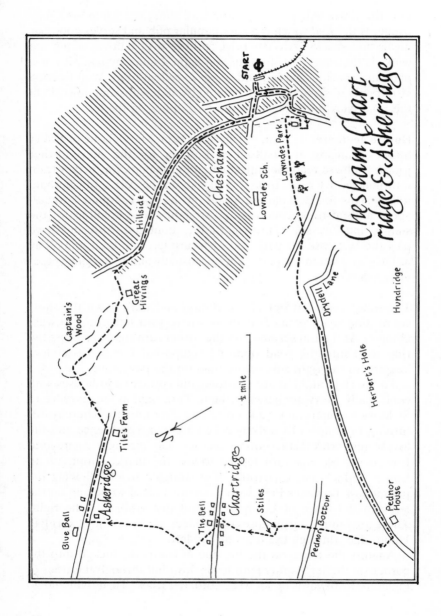

into the town. About a ⅓ of the way along the route, at Chartridge, is the *Bell* which is a very popular pub and serves good bar meals and snacks. At Asheridge, a little over halfway along the walk, is the *Blue Ball*. Its situation is on a quiet by-lane, it has a pleasant, spacious garden and serves excellent food. Well worth a visit if only to slake the thirst created by all the ups and downs! On the road back into Chesham, the *Griffin* lies on the left.

How to get there: By train to Chesham from Marylebone or Baker Street, changing at Chalfont & Latimer for the short further journey; please read the Introduction to the book for further train information. By road, from Amersham on the A416. In Chesham follow signs for Berkhamsted, still on the A416, round 1 roundabout and, at the second one, go straight ahead uphill as for the station and Ley Hill. Turn right after about 200 yards and drive past the Waitrose car park and then turn left into the roomy 'Pay & Display' station car park. There is usually ample parking space. GR: 966/016

The walk: Turn left out of the station and walk down the short connecting road to the Broadway where turn left again to walk along it. At the Barber Shop on the corner turn right and cross the ring road into the road opposite signposted Great Missenden, keeping to the right side of the road on the pavement.

To the right and left are charming old cottages and houses with cool, shady alleyways between them. Turn right at the entrance to St Mary's church and walk up to the gate into the churchyard, turning right again to walk between a green metal fence and the lovely red brick 18th century rectory. Go through a gate into Lowndes Park and turn left to follow the marked footpath to Lower Pednor and Chartridge. Go straight ahead following the path across Lowndes Park with a narrow belt of woodland on the left and the fence of Lowndes School just visible on the right. There are tantalising glimpses of the steep ascent to the next ridge, Hundridge, through the trees on the left.

Against the fence on the far side of the park, tucked into the corner on the left, a tiny path leads downhill through the trees to meet up, in 10 yards or so, with a broader track. Turn right and go

over 2 stiles to emerge again into open country. Here is a marvellous example of a 'dry' valley, Herbert's Hole, with hills rising
steeply on each side of it. These ridges and valleys are very
common features of the Chiltern landscape. Geologists assume
that they were formed at the thawing of the Ice Age when torrents
of water surged down from the north to meet a 'permafrost' in the
chalky Chilterns. The water gouged huge, deep scours making its
way to the clay soil to form rivers such as the Thames. The chalk,
meantime, quickly absorbed the residual water leaving behind
deep dry valleys between high ridges and emerging at the clay line
in the form of springs or tiny rivers, such as the Chess on which
Chesham stands.

Cross the field ahead to a lane and cross it to take the righthand
path across the next field toward Friars Hill and Dry Dell Lane.
Wooded hills dominate the skyline to the right while a great sweep
of pasture drops downhill to the left, the fields delineated by tall
hedges and trees whose shadows pattern the ploughland in the
autumn and winter. Cross stiles and follow the path over fields till
it levels off parallel with the lane and here turn right onto the lane,
following it in the same direction with a view of the sparse line of
cottages at Chartridge on the hilltop on the right. Pheasants scuttle
about the lane and rustle among the leaves of the hedge bottom for
their winter food store. The hamlet of Pednor Bottom lies hidden
in the valley. There are large, isolated houses interspersed with
paddocks of majestic horses.

After 1½ miles the impressive courtyard of Pednor House is
reached between 4 tall round brick pillars. It is a beautiful 16th
century manor of warm red brick and timber with a splendid
carved wooden door in a heavy carved frame. The courtyard
surrounds it and a barn of brick and timber 20 metres long. Twenty
yards on down the lane take the marked path on the right and
follow arrows over stiles and across fields to Pednor Bottom. Cross
the lane here and take the scruffy path opposite, going steeply
uphill to the right of a metal gate. Pause at the stile at the top to
admire yet another 'dry' valley and its accompanying ridges, cattle
grazing peacefully on the sloping hillside and the tiny lane winding
uphill opposite.

Cross the next field and turn left over the stile at the top and, after 20 yards, go over a stile on the right and walk down the field to a stile in the hedge ahead to emerge into the road at Chartridge opposite the *Bell*. Turn left and cross the road after a few yards to take the marked path alongside Chartridge Mission Church on the right. Soon the path bears right between hedges; follow the narrow path ahead as it winds down and uphill, trusses of ripe autumn blackberries tangling the hair, and on into open country. Notice the sensuous curve of the ploughed field to the left. Follow the field edge to the corner of the woodland and then go straight ahead across the field to the point where the hedge opposite comes in on the left. Follow the field edge again, keeping the hedge on the left, to the lane at Asheridge, a tiny hamlet of brick and flint cottages and prosperous farms. About 30 yards to the left is the *Blue Ball*.

Turn right onto the lane and walk down it with marvellous open views on the left. About 30 yards past the entrance to Tiles Farm on the right, take the marked path on the left over a stile and walk down the field ahead toward Captain's Wood. The hedge on the right is colourful in the autumn, tangled with scarlet dog rose and dogwood berries. Go over a stile at the end of the field and soon turn right to follow a broad, easy path through the beechwood, the tall, grey-green trunks striding dramatically downhill on the right. The autumn sun through them dapples the golds and browns of the dying and changing leaves; in the spring the acid green of those same leaves, newborn, forms a perfect backdrop to the carpet of bluebells which covers the floor of the wood.

After about ¾ mile the wooded path reaches a road at Great Hivings and here keep right, following the path parallel with the road. Where the path ends at a road junction, 'Hillside', cross over to walk on the pavement on the left side, following this pleasant suburban road into Chesham town centre. Turn right at the junction with the busy ring road and cross it by means of a subway and go on to the roundabout about 20 yards ahead. Turn left at the roundabout for the station. Just past the public library on the left is a lane leading to Elgiva Hall which has a small snack bar where very welcome cups of tea or coffee are served either indoors or out. Walk down the road ahead to reach the Broadway again, turn right and cross the road to the lane up to the station opposite Boots.

Historical notes

Chesham is an historic little town lying at the source of the river Chess. There is evidence here of Roman settlement and a 7th century Saxon town. Around the large church of St Mary, above the river in the grounds of Chesham Park, huddle picturesque Georgian timber-framed houses and cottages. St Mary's church is of flint with a puddingstone base, a central tower and a slim octagonal spire. Nearby is The Bury, built for William Lowndes, Secretary of the Treasury, in 1712. It is a tall brick house with quoins and a parapet and has 2 little lodges opening onto Church Street. In the Broadway, Arthur Liberty once ran a thriving drapery store before setting up his now famous establishment in Regent Street. The family still lives nearby at The Lee.

Chesham, Ley Hill and Latimer

Introduction: The walk starts in the busy but charming little town of Chesham on the river Chess and follows an uphill route behind small houses, over fields and through woodland to Ley Hill, 600 ft above sea level and an ancient hill settlement. The walk then meanders gently downhill to the outskirts of the village of Latimer and returns to Chesham following the route of the recently developed Chess Valley Walk.

Distance: 8½ to 9 miles – a good day's walking. There are some quite steep climbs to Ley Hill but the return, much of it along the banks of the little river Chess, is level and quite easy going. OS Landranger Map Sheet 165 Aylesbury & Leighton Buzzard.

Refreshments: There are plenty of pubs in Chesham and there are 2, side by side, at Ley Hill; the *Crown* and the *Swan*. Both pubs serve bar meals and have pleasant gardens. At Waterside, on the return route through Chesham, the *Rose & Crown* lies on the right almost opposite the *Elephant & Castle* on the left.

How to get there: By train from Marylebone or Baker Street changing at Chalfont & Latimer Station for Chesham – about 8 minutes journey on; for further information on trains, please read the Introduction to the book. By road, from Amersham on the A416. In Chesham follow the route for Berkhamsted, still the A416, round 1 roundabout and, at the second roundabout, go straight ahead uphill as for the station and Ley Hill. Turn right after about 200 yards and drive past Waitrose car-park and then turn left into the spacious 'Pay & Display' car park near the station. There is usually ample space. GR: 966/016

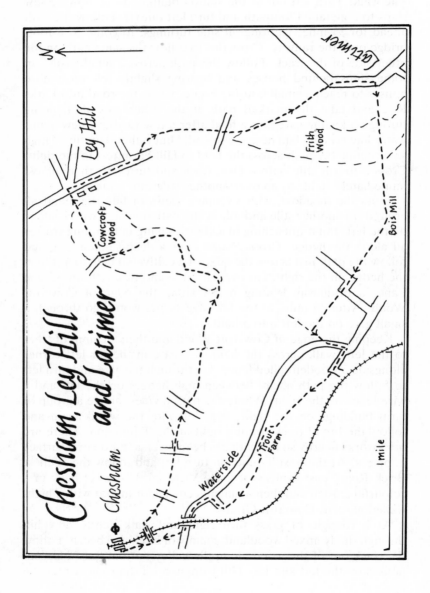

Chesham, Ley Hill and Latimer

The walk: Turn left out of the station building to go down a few steps to a metalled footpath and turn left onto it. Follow the path ahead for ¼ mile, ignoring all side turnings, to come to a footbridge over the railway. Cross this to follow the same path on the other side of the track. Follow this path across 2 small roads, up some steps behind houses and bearing slightly left past more houses to reach a small housing estate. Cross the road into Larks Rise and take the marked path at the other end of it, going through a kissing gate into a field after a few yards. A new mains water line is being laid here, so splendid but rather dauntingly high stiles define the path across the field to Hill Farm just to the right. Cross a fourth stile onto a farm track and turn left, then almost immediately right, to go over another stile into a meadow.

Cross the meadow, with sweeping views of hilly farmland all around, to another stile and follow the path downhill with a hedge on the left; thirst-quenching blackberries hang in tempting trusses all along the hedge. Cross 2 stiles over a deep-sunken lane and follow the path just across the edge of a cultivated field to a stile in the hedge on the right. Go over the stile and turn left into Green Lane, a bridleway leading uphill along the edge of Cowcroft Wood. After ½ mile, at the far edge of the wood, go through a small gate on the left into a field.

Keeping the edge of Cowcroft Wood and then a clump of trees to the left, walk across the field to a gate in the far left corner alongside a wooden railed fence. Go through the gate and turn left to follow the path ahead between high hedges on the left and a wire fence on the right. Where the path divides, above a group of farm buildings on the right, bear left into the wood again and follow the broad track turning right at the T-junction. There are brickworks nearby so the path has been given a 'hard-core' surface in places. At the next T-junction turn left and follow the 'Yellow Brick Road' past a pleasant early Victorian house set back in a colourful garden and then a magnificent Tudor manor with a high-walled garden, Cowcroft Grange.

At a triangle of grass turn right and walk gently downhill through shady mixed woodland, mainly of birch and beech. Follow the track out of the wood along the valley bottom, past pleasant houses on the left and Ley Hill Common on the right. Enter the village at the top of this lane, Kiln Lane, with the *Crown* and the *Swan* on the right to provide welcome refreshment.

Turn right to walk down the lane past the fronts of the pubs and a lawn-mower shop and, just past a turning on the left which appears soon, cross a stile onto a marked footpath concealed in the hedge on the left. Walk over the field alongside a narrow brake of trees and then a hedge on the left; cross the stile at the field edge into another field. At the top of this field turn left through a gap in the hedge and then right to come out into a lane. Cross the lane to a marked path opposite, walking for a few yards parallel with the lane and then turning right onto a well-defined path through Codmore Wood. At a path junction, opposite a notice barring public access, turn left onto a broad path through mixed woodland of beech, birch and oak trees. Soon a gravelled driveway is crossed and, after about another 250–300 yards on the path, strike off to the left on a path 10 yards from the wood edge.

Go over a stile into a large field and carry on straight ahead across it to a gap in the hedge on the far side, emerging onto a lane. Turn right and walk downhill for ⅓ mile to a large house. Just before the house take the marked footpath on the right, up paving stones and over a stile. (If you want to see Latimer, which is a charming tiny hamlet, keep on down the lane past the house for another ⅓ mile and then take the Chess Valley Walk path past the beautiful early 18th century Old Rectory and just past Latimer Cottage, where the path lies on the left and leads across a field into the village.) Turn left to pass the back of the large house and then right and left to skirt the wood edge on a well-trodden path with open farmland on the right. At the field corner the path enters the wood to the left for a few yards and emerges onto the steep scarp of the hill overlooking the valley of the Chess with the little river wandering drunkenly below. The path continues down alongside the wood on the right with, in the late summer, scarlet and black berries of wild viburnum and whitebeam making a striking contrast at its edge.

Go through a gate at the wood end into open fields to Blackwell Farm, where turn left to follow the sign for the Chess Valley Walk and another sign on the right after 20 yards alongside a walled garden with a lavender hedge.

Go over the stile at the end and follow the path over stiles and across meadows until a broad track with Chess Valley Walk signs on a post is reached, close to the road. Turn left to the road and left again to walk along it to another Chess Valley Walk sign on the right after about 50 yards. This leads into a lane which runs alongside the now fast-flowing river, with watercress beds at its edges and some quite large fish in its middle. Where the lane curves sharply left go straight ahead on the path between hedges and over a stile into a field, keeping the river beyond the hedge on the right. Soon, at a kissing gate on the right, there is another Chess Valley Walk sign; go through the gate and follow a narrow path crossing the river and alongside a newly made trout farm. Moorhens, ducks and swans swim around or sit comfortably on the many grassy islets on the left. When the path appears to be totally blocked by high wire-mesh fencing, sneak beside it to the left and follow the path along the other side of the trout farm and turn right at the end to go over a footbridge.

Over the bridge turn left to follow the path alongside the river again, soon crossing it by a little waterfall, and follow the path ahead with water now on both sides. Pleasant gardens run down to the river on the right. Soon the path comes into a large recreation ground on the left; walk ahead to the road leaving the recreation ground by a small footbridge and turn right to walk up to the main road at Waterside. Turn left and cross the road to make use of the pavement on the other side and walk back into the town, with the *Rose & Crown* pub on the right almost opposite the *Elephant & Castle* on the left. Go under a railway bridge and quite soon turn right into Punch Bowl Lane which leads onto the original path from the station. Turn left to follow the path back to the station or car park.

Historical notes

Chesham, an historic little town, lies at the source of the river Chess and has a long connection with manufacture based on mills at Waterside. There is evidence here of Roman settlement and a 7th century Saxon town. Around the large church of St Mary, above the river in the grounds of Chesham Park, huddle pictures-

31

que timber-framed houses and attractive Georgian cottages. The church is of flint with a puddingstone base, a central tower and a slim octagonal spire. Nearby is The Bury, built for William Lowndes in 1712; it is a tall brick house with quoins and a parapet. It has 2 little lodges opening onto Church Street. The other, Waterside, end of the town is a hotch-potch of small factories and early 18th century cottages but soon gives way to the more picturesque old mills and the remains of the watercress beds for which the town was once famous. In the Broadway, Arthur Liberty once ran a thriving drapery store before setting up his now famous establishment in Regent Street. The family still lives nearby at The Lee.

Ley Hill had a reputation for drunkenness in its earlier years because of the proximity of the 4 public houses in its parish. The common also provided good camping ground for gypsies, who made pegs from the abundant growths of hazel there. Brickmaking has been a local industry for many years; nowadays the bricks are machine-made and no longer made by hand.

Latimer: This delightful and peaceful village, just ¼ mile off the walk, is centred round a small green on which stands the village pump, in use until 50 years ago when mains water came to the village. A strange obelisk nearby honours the local men who fought in the Boer War and beside it is a stone with plaques in memory of the horse ridden by General de Villebois Mareuil at the battle of Boshof in April 1900. The General was killed but the horse survived to be brought to England by Major General Lord Chesham. It died in February 1911. The green is surrounded by pretty 17th and 18th century cottages. In the park is Latimer House, rebuilt by Blore in 1863 as a large Tudor mansion of red brick and stone. Part of the Chess in the valley below was dammed to make a tree-fringed lake. The village is well worth a visit, if only for a picnic lunch in the water meadows; it has no pub and no shop!

The Chess Valley Walk is the joint brainchild of the Bucks County Council and the West Herts area of the Countryside Management services. It is waymarked with a trout symbol on a yellow arrow and starts in Chesham itself. Wandering through the Chess valley for 10 miles, it finally merges with the river Colne near Rickmansworth. Only a small part is walked here but there is opportunity to observe the varied wildlife along the way; kingfishers and herons are often seen near the water and moorhens, ducks and swans nest on the islets or the banks of the river. Dragonflies can be seen hovering on hot summer days and trout are plentiful. The trout farm on the walk lies on Chesham Moor where the first mill was built by Lady Elgive in the 10th century. She had the river diverted to create the Moor, in fact a large island. Watercress was grown around the Moor commercially until recently.

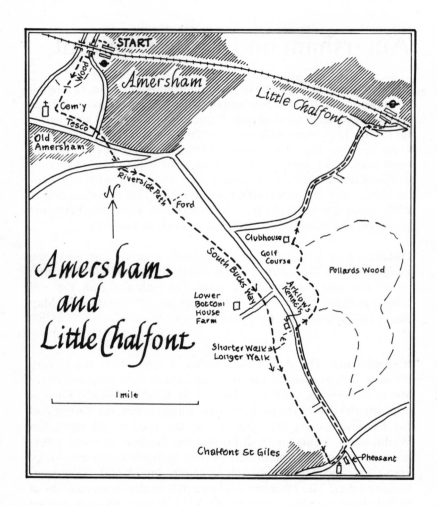

Amersham and Little Chalfont

Introduction: The walk starts downhill from Amersham, through a beechwood and into the Misbourne valley, where it traverses fields and water meadows, passes small thickets of woodland and peaceful farms. The longer walk emerges into the village of Chalfont St Giles opposite the village green. Milton's cottage lies just up the road to the right, on the left-hand side. The way to Little Chalfont lies between a large mixed wood and a golf course, with spectacular views over the surrounding countryside. This is not a circular walk, but a train from Little Chalfont station will easily transport you back to Amersham for the car or back to London.

Distance: 8 or 6 miles. Most of the walk is gentle and easy; the greatest hazard the walker faces is that of flying golf balls whizzing out of the rough alongside the path! The path alongside the golf course is uphill but not too strenuously so. OS Landranger Map Sheet 165 Aylesbury & Leighton Buzzard. Pathfinder Sheet SU89/99.

Refreshments: The new Tesco stores in Amersham has a very pleasant little restaurant for coffee and tea or light lunches. There are a number of pubs in Chalfont St Giles; *Merlin's Cave* is opposite the exit of the path onto the village green, the *Crown* and the *Feathers* are on the same side of the road to the right. On Wednesdays, Thursdays and Fridays the *Feathers* provides afternoon teas, but don't be misled by The Stratton Tearooms – they aren't any more but only sell delicious bread and appetising-looking cakes! The *Pheasant* is a large pub on the crossroads about ¼ mile from the village toward the A413. It has a pleasant garden and a play area for children. In Little Chalfont, the *Sugar Loaves* near the station offers bar meals.

How to get there: By train to Amersham from Marylebone or Baker Street; please read the Introduction to the book for further train information. By road on the M40 to Beaconsfield then the A355 to Amersham, where it is advisable to park in the car park off the main street on the right just past the bus and coach station. A short walk through the car park and over a tiny bridge brings the walker onto the path from the station where turn right to follow the route. GR: 964/981

The walk: Turn left to walk down from the station and left again under the railway bridge. Cross the road to take the footpath opposite between new houses and the railway line and, after 20 yards, bear a little left onto a broad path through the wood parallel with a minor road on the right. Follow the path straight downhill and across a large cultivated field. At the field end turn left and follow the path for about ¼ mile past a small cemetery, a large field and the new Tesco stores on the right. At the end of the path cross Station Road to a path opposite and cross the next road to take a path opposite over a stile. Follow this path, meandering along beside the river Misbourne, through a bridge under the bypass and straight ahead with views over the fields to the left and the river on the right; beyond it the ground rises steeply to a wooded crown.

After about ½ mile cross a bridge/ford on the right and follow the path ahead, which turns abruptly left after about 10 yards and carries on over grass fields approached by stiles. On the far side of the third field is a lane which cross to continue along the path now signposted 'South Bucks Way'. Over the next stile the path turns right alongside the field for a few yards and then turns left alongside a fence. Go over the next stile into a small wood.

For the SHORTER WALK, take a small path on the left just inside the wood and follow it alongside the wood with a fence on the right. Go over a stile at the far end of the wood and cross the grass field to a stile in the lefthand corner to emerge onto the A413, with Arklow's Kennels on the left and the path uphill round the golf course immediately opposite. Continue at * below.

For the LONGER WALK continue on the broad path with open fields now on the left looking toward the busy road and wooded hills beyond. Just before entering the village of Chalfont St Giles the path traverses a few yards of metalled lane alongside Chalfont Mill and Mill Farm and then a gravelled lane behind houses to emerge into the village opposite the green and the church. The village is worth exploring; Milton's cottage lies up the main street on the lefthand side and is a little museum of Milton memorabilia. The *Pheasant* pub lies about ¼ mile to the left of the exit of the South Bucks Way. To continue the walk, the walker must make a choice; either to retrace the South Bucks Way back to the small brake of trees, now on the right, and take the narrow path down through the wood following the route of the shorter walk, or to walk a short mile along the A413, which has a pathway and a wide grass verge on its right side, back toward Amersham by turning left opposite the *Pheasant*. Walk along the road on the verge until Arklow's Kennels, on the left side of the road, is reached.

*Rejoin the route of the shorter walk and take the marked footpath on the right leading to the edge of the golf course. The path dodges in and out of Pollards Wood, a beautiful mixed woodland of beech, birch, oak and ash with lovely autumnal splashes of colour made by the crimsons and golds of wild cherry trees and bright scarlet crab-apples which, so country people say, are not as flavoursome for jelly as their duller-coloured green-gold cousins. Tall skeletons of cow parsley stand starkly against the sky on the rough grassy edges of course and wood. Crimson bramble leaves are entwined with purple-black spindle and scarlet rose hips. The path climbs gently uphill, hugging the wood edge and turning right with it opposite the clubhouse on the far side of the course. Here is a marvellous point to stop and drink in the view; the water tower at Coleshill is plainly visible high on its hilltop to the left and the beautiful rolling tree-studded countryside lies between. Lower Bottom House Farm is in the valley opposite, sheltered by the dense clump of High Wood behind it.

The path actually passes straight across the new part of the golf course from this corner but it is wisest to stick to the edge of the wood until a fence is reached.

Walk alongside the fence across the top of the course to reach a gap in the hedge with metal bars across it and here enter a narrow path between high fences which emerges onto a lane where keep straight ahead. The lane goes past some pleasant houses and gardens and bears right opposite the warm red-brick and timber-framed barn of Cokes Farm. Cross the road at the T-junction to turn left and walk on the pavement of Cokes Lane. In the spring the gardens alongside the road are colourful with blossoming shrubs and wide tulip beds and in the autumn the colours of dying and changing leaves and berries on the shrubs are beautiful. In ½ mile Little Chalfont village is reached. At the T-junction turn right past the shops along Chalfont Station Road and cross it at the lighted pedestrian crossing. The *Sugar Loaves* pub is close to the crossing, where turn left to find the station, crossing the line by subway for the London train platform.

Historical notes

Amersham-on-the-Hill was created around the turn of the century when the Metropolitan Railway extended its route past Little Chalfont to Amersham and Aylesbury. It is separated from, and 60 metres higher than, the old town and stands above flinty sloping fields edged with beechwoods. The town has spread a great deal since the Second World War, with ribbon development occurring much of the way along the A413 toward Chalfont St Giles. The valley of the Misbourne, so-called because of its propensity to dry up (now you see it, now you don't), remains peacefully meandering through low-lying arable and cultivated farmland.

Chalfont St Giles' Norman church, dedicated to St Giles, patron saint of woodland, is approached through a timber-framed lych-gate under a timber-framed house. Much of the church interior is of 13th century origin but the exterior was overly Victorianised by Street in 1863. Among the wall paintings are 14th century scenes from the life of the Virgin Mary and of Jesus Christ. The early 18th century rectory, which has carved brackets and columns to its doorcase, lies to the north-west of the church.

Milton's Cottage, though in fact Milton himself never owned it, was built by the Fleetwood family who owned a large estate, The

Vache, to the east of the village. In 1665, when the plague overtook London, Milton sought refuge in the country and his friend, Thomas Ellwood, found and rented the cottage on Milton's behalf. Ellwood was imprisoned for his Quaker beliefs but was released in time to visit Milton in the cottage and receive from him the completed manuscript of *Paradise Lost*. The cottage was purchased by public subscription in 1887 in honour of the Queen's Jubilee.

Little Chalfont: On the road which once joined Reading to Hatfield, Little Chalfont was no more than a group of isolated farms – Burton's, Coke's and Nightingales, until the coming of the railway in 1890. Burton's Farm was mentioned in the Domesday Book. Nowadays the village is a pleasant suburban extension of Amersham-on-the-Hill.

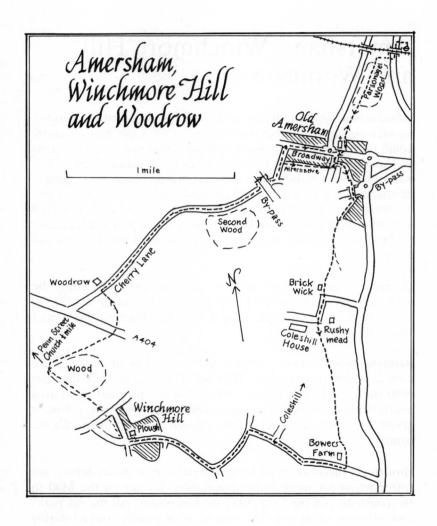

Amersham,
Winchmore Hill
and Woodrow

1 mile

Amersham, Winchmore Hill and Woodrow

Introduction: A stimulating and varied walk starting downhill through beechwoods from the station to Old Amersham. A climb uphill through rolling open countryside brings you to the outskirts of Coleshill village and by small lanes to Winchmore Hill. The walk traverses a wood where a border of wild cherry trees blooms profusely in the spring and crosses fields and a road to a lane into the little hamlet of Woodrow. From there it is a gentle downhill walk on a quiet and narrow lane, crossing the bypass and returning to Amersham station along the lovely old high street of the old town.

Distance: A good 7 miles so allow at least 3 hours to enjoy the walk, absorb the views and stop for refreshment en route. OS Landranger Sheet 165 Aylesbury & Leighton Buzzard, Pathfinder Sheet SU 89/99.

Refreshments: There are heaps of pubs in Amersham but there are only 2 on the way, both at Winchmore Hill. The walk emerges onto the road by the *Plough*, which has a a pleasant patio area overlooking the common and serves bar food. The *Potters Arms* is about 200 yards to the left of the *Plough* and also overlooks the common.

How to get there: By train from Marylebone or Baker Street; see Introduction for more train information. By car on the M40 to Beaconsfield and then the A413 to Amersham. All the car parks and adjacent roads near the station are normally packed during the week but can probably be used at weekends. Approaching Amersham there is a large roundabout, part of the new bypass, which cross for the town. At the next roundabout into the Broadway turn right to follow the road to another roundabout, turn left into Station Road. The turning for the car park is on the right just before a railway bridge and is signposted. During the week however it would be as well to turn left into the high street and make use of the large 'Pay & Display' car park on the right just past the bus station. On leaving the car park turn right and walk up the high street to the church, where you join the walk. GR: 964 981

The walk: Turn left out of the station and left again to go under the railway bridge. Cross the road here to take the path opposite between new houses and the railway line and, after 20 yards, bear a little left onto a broad path through the wood, walking parallel with a minor road on the right. Follow the path straight down hill and across a large cultivated field. At the field end turn left and then right over a small brick bridge over the infant river Misbourne. Walk ahead through the churchyard, keeping the large church of St Mary on the right, and come out into the high street opposite the Griffin Hotel, of 17th century origin.

Cross the Broadway at the pedestrian crossing and turn left into Wheilden Street. After about 50 yards turn left again into Wheilden Green and go over a stile on the right at the top to cross a small field. Go over another stile and follow a narrow path straight into a small housing estate. Turn right and take the metalled footpath ahead, turning right and then left to cross a splendid footbridge over the bypass. Go over the field ahead and turn right onto a marked path which runs behind a line of houses and then straight ahead uphill between steep curves of hills with a deep ditch on the right of the path.

At a path intersection coming in on the left, cross to the other side of the hedge just before a large ash tree; now the deep ditch and hedge are on the left. Go on uphill passing a charming little house, 'Brick Wick', on the right. Pause here to turn round and absorb the splendid views down and uphill on each side of the Misbourne valley in which Old Amersham lies. Go on up the shady flint track to emerge onto a lane. Turn right, walk down for about 150 yards and, just behind the 'Coleshill' sign, take the footpath through a metal gate on the left by the entrance to Rushymead Lodge. Follow the well-defined path down and uphill over stiles and across grass and cornfields until the path becomes a gravel track turning to the right. Here go on ahead across the field toward Bowers Farm where the path bears left to skirt the farmhouse and goes over 2 more stiles on each side of a small paddock to emerge onto a lane. There are wonderful views of sweeping country bordered by thickset deciduous woodland all along this part of the walk. In the summer peacock, orange-tip and tiny blue chalk butterflies flitter about the fields.

Turn right onto the lane and walk up it for a good ½ mile noticing, as you pass, a beautiful clematis spread across the front of a flint cottage on the left and, very soon, the square facade of the Georgian mansion, Coleshill House. Cross the road on the right leading to Coleshill village and go on up the lane into Winchmore Hill, ignoring the turning on the right and bearing right at the T-junction opposite a red brick house.

The fields are soon left behind and small houses appear on both sides and then the grand edifice, the *Plough*, appears on the right. Walk across the road in front of the *Plough* and another, minor, road and walk to the right down the length of the common to its far right corner. Cross the road to a marked footpath opposite between well-tended allotments on the left and wide, tree-bordered views on the right. Go over a stile and cross the field to another stile into a wood where the wild cherry trees blossom cheerfully in the spring. Follow the broad path ahead into open country with a view of the spire of Penn Street church across the field.

Turn right at the wood edge and right again after a few yards following the wood edge and on alongside cultivated fields with a thickset hedge on the right, to emerge finally onto the A404 just past a large barn on the right. Cross the road to a narrow lane signposted 'Woodrow' and follow this for about ¼ mile to a T-junction where turn right into Cherry Lane.

Walk on down this lovely quiet lane, with open views all around, for about 2 miles passing Secondwood Farm on the left and picking, if you wish, the abundant luscious blackberries in the hedge on the right; honeysuckle and dog roses bloom in the hedge in early summer. The lane comes to a dead end at the bypass so here turn left to follow the path between a small copse on the left and a fence on the right. The path leads down a gentle slope to the edge of the bypass. Visibility is good here but cross the bypass with care to the marked path opposite and follow this path gently uphill again. After about 200 yards, at a path sign leading over a field, take a track on the left to walk gently downhill to Amersham's Broadway at its top end. Turn right to follow the road back to the church and uphill to the station again. Alternatively there is a marked footpath on the right toward the bottom of the track which borders the houses and gardens of the town and emerges finally into Wheilden Street again. Turn left at the path end to walk back to the Broadway and the church.

Historical notes

Amersham lies on the medieval route to Aylesbury through the Wendover Gap in the Chilterns and is steeped in history. Every building in the main street, called Broadway, is beautiful; until 30 years ago it was narrowed at its London end by an island of cottages and a market square. The Market Hall, a 2-storey red brick and stone building with a white cupola, was built for the Drakes of Shardeloes. Bury Farm was the home of Mary Pennington and Guilielma Springett, wife of William Penn. There are three noteworthy houses among the predominantly 17th/18th century buildings in Broadway; No 47 is an original 15th century 3-gabled house, Elmondesham House is a 3-storied building with 11 bays of purple and red brick, and the Drake Almshouse was built in 1657. The *Crown Hotel* has a columned porch and courtyard and the *Kings Arms* has a wealth of timber gables. Now that the town is bypassed it is a great pleasure to walk leisuredly along this lovely street to admire the warm red brick and timber architecture.

Bowers Farm was built by George Coleshill in 1614, on the site of a medieval manor, Stockbury. It has, it is reputed, the oldest oven in Bucks, panelled walls and a cased staircase for the servants; they could retreat to their bedrooms without being privy to the goings-on of the family!

Penn Street's Holy Trinity church, whose spire can be observed on this walk, is said to have been built at the suggestion of Queen Adelaide during a visit to Penn House. She thought it an idyllic place for a church, so there it is. The church has an octagonal tower and the spire, of oak shingle, is 150 ft high.

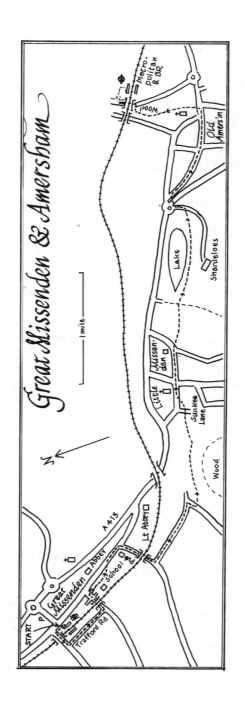

Great Missenden to Amersham

Introduction: This is a pleasant and undemanding walk, with no strenuous hill-climbing to do. An old footpath leads from Great Missenden to the lane up to Little Kingshill, and there are magnificent sweeping views on both sides of the path along the ridge leading into Little Missenden, tucked away from traffic and almost seeming not to belong to the 20th century. The path then leads through fields alongside a stream and the man-made lakes at Shardeloes to emerge across the cricket field and the new bypass into the town of Amersham, a charming hotch-potch of houses and cottages dating from the 15th to the 19th century. Very little of the 20th century obtrudes here and, now that the town is bypassed, it is indeed a pleasant stroll along its high street to the church and up across the field and woods behind it to the station to catch a train back to London or to Great Missenden. This is not a round walk but, for the truly dedicated walker, the next walk offers a way back to Great Missenden by another route.

Distance: 7 miles – allow 3½ to 4 hours; it would be a pity to rush relentlessly through this lovely bit of Chiltern countryside. OS Map Sheet 165 Aylesbury & Leighton Buzzard. Pathfinder Sheet SP 80/90.

Refreshments: There are plenty of pubs in Great Missenden itself and after the first mile or so the walker might be tempted into the *Nag's Head* where excellent bar snacks and meals are available. In Little Missenden there are 2 pubs; the *Crown*, quite near the manor, and the *Red Lion* at the far end of the village. Both serve bar snacks. In Amersham the choice is bewildering with pubs, large and small, on both sides of the high street, some of which have restaurants as well as bar service for snacks.

How to get there: By train from Marylebone in 45 minutes through good countryside. Please read the Introduction to the book for further train information. By road on the M40 to Beaconsfield and A413 as for Aylesbury. At Great Missenden, about 7 miles from Amersham, at the second roundabout turn left and there is shortly a large 'Pay & Display' car park on the right. On leaving the car park turn right and cross the High Street into Station Road opposite. Go over the railway bridge and follow the walk from there. GR 894 014

The walk: Walk out of the station yard and turn left to cross the railway bridge to take the marked path on the left, Trafford Road, and go straight ahead. After ½ mile, at a junction with a lane, turn left onto it to go under a railway bridge and walk on for a few yards. Turn right to walk across the grass in front of some houses to a footpath alongside the Misbourne School and playing fields. Follow this path, with the road parallel on the left, for about ½ mile. The path continues past some tall Victorian villas on the right and then comes down onto the road. Walk along the road and turn right off it alongside the *Nag's Head* into Nags Head Lane. Keep to the footpath under the railway bridge and then turn left up the hill. There is a footpath on the other side of the lane for a short distance but, when the path peters out, it is wise to keep well in on this narrow, fairly busy lane; the path reappears at the top of the hill. Bear right and very soon the marked public footpath, on the opposite side of the road, appears by a lay-by just past a bus stop.

Take this path through a little strip of woodland and over a stile into open country. A well-defined path along the ridge of hill gives splendid sweeping views of rolling farmland and woods falling and rising all around. Larks rise, calling, over the fields and greenfinches nest in the hedge ahead. Follow the path through the hedge, over a stile and across a field to a pair of stiles on either side of an old, deeply sunken lane. Cross both stiles into a paddock and walk diagonally across it to the houses in the right hand corner, where there is a stile onto the road into Little Missenden.

On the left is the tiny river Misbourne which, as often as not, is dried up. The field edge near the church is bright with a carpet of snowdrops in the spring. The church lies a little back from the road on the left and, if you are lucky enough to find a flower-arranger or a 'Holy Duster' at work inside, it is well worth a look round. Follow the road to come to the beautiful Jacobean manor house on the left, seen through high wrought-iron gates. Keep on down the road ignoring turnings to right and left. Shortly after the *Red Lion* the road bends sharply to the left to reach the main road. Leave it here and go straight ahead through a gate onto a wide track parallel with and above the stream for 1½ miles, crossing 2 stiles. As the river opens out into lakes below Shardeloes, the path bears left toward them to a stile in the corner. There are many varieties of ducks and geese on the lakes and moorhens hug the banks wittering at their young. Go on through the next gate into the cricket field and cross it to the exit of the path onto the drive of Shardeloes. Here turn left to a slip road and cross it to a path opposite which leads to the bypass. This has to be crossed to the path opposite. Do it carefully; visibility is good and the traffic is slowing having come from, or going to, the roundabout but you might need the assistance of a 'lollipop lady' at 5.30 on a Friday afternoon.

Follow the path ahead into Amersham with its multitude of pubs on either side of the high street. The *Crown* has an interesting columned porch and courtyard and the *Kings Arms* huge timbered gables. Cross the road near the Market Hall and walk to the church. Turn left into the churchyard and follow the path, leaving the church on the left, onto a small cross-path with a tiny bridge to the left over the infant river Misbourne. Take the path ahead straight uphill across a huge field and into a wood. Follow the path up through the wood with a minor road on the left. At the top of the wood turn right onto a metalled path beside some modern houses. The path emerges onto Station Road. Cross to go under the railway bridge and turn right to the station.

Historical notes

Great Missenden Abbey was founded by William de Missenden in 1133 but was dissolved by Henry VIII in 1534. The estate was finally purchased by a London ironmonger, John Oldham in 1783 and a Venetian-style house was built on the site of the old abbey with later additions of neo-Gothic castellations and a central, castellated pediment. The house stands among huge cedars in a park-like landscape opposite the Misbourne School and is now an Adult Education Centre.

There is said to be a secret passage, which no one has ever found, connecting Great Missenden Abbey with Little Missenden Abbey some ¾ mile along the same road; its gatehouse can just be seen from the *Nag's Head*. From its dissolution the Little Abbey has been successively a private dwelling, a school for maladjusted children, an hotel and now, with modern additions, is a prestigious private hospital.

The church of St Peter and St Paul is cut off from the village by the bypass and stands high above it on a hillside on the left.

Little Missenden: The church of St John the Baptist is of 12th century origin but additions were made in the 13th century. In the 14th century the north chapel was added and the timbered porch is of the 15th century. There are 2 important wall paintings, discovered in 1931, of the 13th century and depicting St Christopher with the Child Jesus and St Catherine.

In October each year the village holds a Festival of Arts and the works of contemporary composers such as Michael Tippett and Edmund Rubbra are performed. Both these composers had close connections with Little Missenden Abbey while it was a school for 'difficult' children run on the lines of A.S. Neill's school in Sussex. Michael Tippett taught at the school for a short time and Rubbra, whose piano was housed in the school, often visited. On one occasion he sat at the piano to play one of his recent compositions, to be told, at its end, that 'that wasn't bad for a tramp' by a small schoolgirl.

Amersham: Shardeloes was built in 1776 by Stiff Leadbetter and altered later by Robert Adam. It is a large, square house whose giant portico faces north across the valley. The interiors, part Adam and part by James Wyatt, are now converted to flats and maisonettes. The grounds and lakes were designed by Humphry Repton.

Three interesting houses in the High Street are worth noting: No 47 is a 15th century 3-gabled house, Elmondesham House is a 3-storied building with 11 bays of purple and red brick, and the Drake Almshouse was built in 1657. In Wheilden Street, buried among a jumble of hospital buildings and a hideous 11-storey block, is the old Tudor-style workhouse built by G.G. Scott in 1838. Nearby is the Friends Meeting House of 1685, plain and unadorned as one would expect.

Amersham-on-the-Hill, the new town, was built between the wars around the railway station and extends now almost to Little Chalfont. Here there are examples of the extravagantly 'modern' building styles of the early 1930s, and some houses which try to be more 'Tudor' than the genuine ones down the hill in the old town.

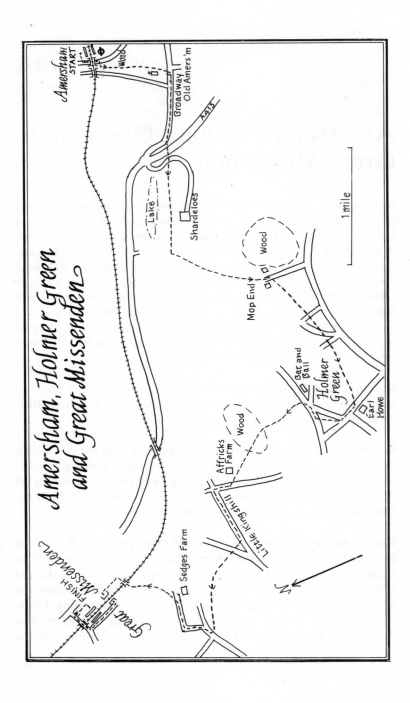

Amersham, Holmer Green
and Great Missenden

Amersham
START

Wood

Broadway
Old Amers Im

A413

Lake

Shardeloes

1 mile

Wood

Mop End

Wood

Bat and
Ball

Holmer
Green

Earl
Howe

Affricks
Farm

Wood

Little Kingshill

Sedges Farm

Great Missenden

FINISH
Gt Missenden

Amersham, Holmer Green and Great Missenden

Introduction: From Amersham this walk passes through some spectacular hilltop scenery and meanders through the village of Holmer Green which, like Topsy, has 'growed'. There are large new housing developments on the outskirts but the village green is surrounded by old flint and brick houses and cottages. The walk takes a downhill track through woodland past Affricks Farm to Little Kingshill, a long thin village, and then through more woodland via Sedges Farm back to Great Missenden. This is not a circular walk but the return journey to Amersham can be made by train. Alternatively you can walk back to Amersham by a different route, using the directions in Walk Seven.

Distance: 10 miles from Amersham station. Allow 3 to 4 hours to enjoy the walk. OS Map Sheet 165 Aylesbury & Leighton Buzzard. Pathfinder Sheet SU 89/99.

Refreshments: There are a number of pubs in Amersham on both sides of the Broadway; at Holmer Green the *Earl Howe* is close to where the path emerges into the village and the *Bat & Ball* is on the right hand corner of the village green alongside Penfold Lane. The *Full Moon* at Little Kingshill also serves bar snacks.

How to get there: By train from Marylebone or Baker Street; see Introduction for more train information. By car on the M40 to Beaconsfield and then A413 to Amersham. All the car parks and adjacent roads near the station are normally packed during the week but can probably be used at weekends. Approaching Amersham there is a large roundabout, part of the relatively new bypass, which cross for the town. At the next roundabout into the

Broadway turn right to follow the road to the next roundabout and turn left into Station Road. The turning for the car park is on the right just before a railway bridge and is signposted. During the week it would be as well to turn left into the high street and make use of the large 'Pay & Display' car park on the right just past the bus station. On leaving the car park turn right and walk up the Broadway to the church, where you join the walk. GR: 964 981

The walk: Turn left out of the station and left again to go under the railway bridge. Cross the road here to take the path opposite between new houses and the railway line and, after 20 yards, bear a little left onto a broad path through the wood walking parallel with a minor road on the right. Follow the path straight down hill and across a large cultivated field. At the field end turn left and then right over a small brick bridge over the infant river Misbourne and ahead through the churchyard, keeping the large church of St Mary on the right, and come out into the high street opposite the *Griffin Hotel*, of 17th century origin.

Turn right and walk up the high street past the old Market Hall with the *Crown* and the *King's Arms* opposite and some fascinating little shops on the left. Walk up the road for about ¾ mile with the bypass now running almost parallel with it on the left. Cross the street and walk on the left side and the path will lead leftward toward a crossing of the bypass not far from the roundabout. Visibility is good, though cross with care onto a path on the far side which leads to a slip road to Shardeloes. The lodge and drive lie on the left.

Turn into Shardeloes drive and walk up it for a short ¼ mile and opposite a large white house take a path on the left through a gate. The field on the left rises steeply to a dark backdrop of woods and, in the spring, the path is bordered by big clumps of bluebells. Follow the path straight ahead along the valley ignoring all the side turnings. At a brake of trees beside a wooden 'hide' cross the stile, ignoring the one on the left and walk ahead then bear slightly left. Cross a track which leads into an electricity power station and keep on the marked path along the wood edge on the right and past a house onto the lane at Mop End.

Cross the lane to a stile and go over the field diagonally to another stile across a bridleway into the field opposite. Follow the path straight ahead past a bungalow and a group of flint cottages. Cross the next lane to a path opposite and then another lane to another path opposite leading straight into Holmer Green.

At the T-junction turn right past the *Earl Howe* and right again alongside the duck pond. After 200 yards cross the road and the village green to the *Bat & Ball*. Turn right into Penfold Lane, signposted for Little Missenden. After about 400 yards take the second marked footpath on the left opposite Penfold Cottages. Go over a stile and diagonally across a large field to the left hand corner. Go over the stile there and walk down the field keeping the thick hedge on the left. In summer the hedge is bright with pink dog roses and honeysuckle and in the autumn tempting bunches of luscious blackberries trail from it. Go over a stile at the end of the field and turn half-right, crossing a drive, to a sunken, flinty lane downhill through Haleacre Wood with the wood edge on the left, ignoring all side turnings. There are glimpses of beautiful rolling farmland scenery on the right as the wood is left behind. The track then goes gently uphill past Affricks Farm on the right and finally emerges onto a lane to Little Kingshill.

Turn right and walk up the lane past Boot Farm and at the T-junction turn left to walk into Little Kingshill. Follow the road for a good ½ mile past a school on the right and the village hall on the left. Opposite Kingshill Baptist church, on the far side of a playing field, take the marked path (South Bucks Way) on the right. The *Full Moon* pub is on the road at the top where turn right and then left to take the path past the pub garden and into open country. Walk ahead into devastated Sandwich Wood keeping the wood edge on the left as far as possible; fallen trees are everywhere! At the wood end turn left and take a stile on the right to follow a clearly defined path bearing right across a large cultivated field. At the road turn right into a narrow lane and after 100 yards take the marked track on the left marked Sedges Farm.

Follow the metalled track through Sedges Farm with the house on the right and take a path immediately on the left over a stile and walk across the field to a stile in the right hand corner. Turn left and follow the track downhill and through a gate or stile on the left at the bottom to walk uphill with the hedge and then a fence on the right. On the far side of this large field is another stile which cross and then cross the little footbridge over the railway and follow the path down to a small housing estate. Cross the estate to a lane forming a T-junction and here turn left to go under the railway bridge and then right to follow a track/lane (Trafford Road!) back to the road above Great Missenden station. Turn right out of Trafford Road and cross the railway bridge and turn right into the station itself.

Historical notes

Shardeloes was built in 1776 by Stiff Leadbetter and later altered by Robert Adam. It is a large, square house whose huge portico faces north across the valley. The interiors, part by Adam and part by James Wyatt, are now converted into flats and maisonettes. The grounds and lakes were designed by Humphry Repton.

Three interesting houses in Amersham Broadway are worth noting; No 47 is an original 15th century 3-gabled house, Elmondesham House is a 3-storied building with 11 bays of purple and red brick, and the Drake Almshouse was built in 1657.

Holmer Green: Two features of the Enclosure Act of 1854 are retained in the village. Its village green, Holmer Green Common, which belonged to the lord of the manor, was to be fenced, sheep were to graze it and the populace allowed to play on it. Cricket is still played on it in the summer. The other is the Holmer Pond, dedicated by the Enclosure Act, and now beautifully maintained by a Pond Committee!

Little Kingshill: The origins of the village date back to AD 900 and the founding of a monastery. William I gave a manor and lands to the Earl of Aufrics, hence Affricks Farm, now a modern farmhouse but, in between, a fine Elizabethan manor.

Great Missenden and Prestwood

Introduction: This is a delightful short walk. There are wide airy views from the hilltops as the walk proceeds up to Prestwood and the return down a quiet leafy lane is peaceful and has much of delight upon which to rest the eye. On an autumn afternoon when the evenings are beginning to pull in, the changing colours of the leaves in the woodland and the play of low, golden sunlight through them is magnificent.

Distance: 4 miles – no very demanding climbing and easy-going downhill walking. OS Landranger Map Sheet 165 Aylesbury & Leighton Buzzard. Pathfinder Sheet SP 80/90.

Refreshments: There are a number of pubs in Great Missenden itself offering good bar meals, and the baker's shop on the left hand side of the High Street now serves tea and coffee. The *Green Man* at Prestwood lies about halfway along the walk.

How to get there: By train to Great Missenden from Marylebone or Baker Street. Please read the Introduction to the book for further train information. By road, on the A413 from Amersham toward Aylesbury. At the second roundabout, about 6 miles from Amersham, turn left for Great Missenden and there is a large 'Pay & Display' car park in this slip road on the right. Turn right out of the car park, cross the High Street and join the walk at Trafford Road. GR: 894 014

The walk: Turn left out of the station yard and cross the railway line over a bridge and take the marked path almost immediately on the left, Trafford Road. Go straight ahead for ½ a mile with pleasant small houses set back on the right to a T-junction, where turn right steeply up a lane. After about 50 yards cross a stile on

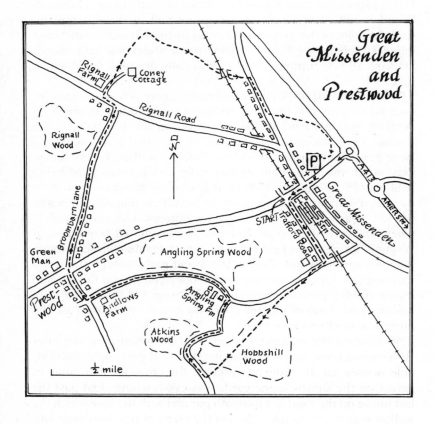

the left onto a well-defined footpath with the high road hedge on the right, followed by a wooden fence, and follow the path ahead to another, very grand, stile into Hobbshill Wood. Pause before entering the wood to look back at the long view over the valley to the wooded hills on the far side and a glimpse of the squat tower of Great Missenden church standing above the little town. Hobbshill Wood is full of bluebells in the spring and in the autumn the sunlight colours the grey-green trunks of the tall old beeches and dapples their fading leaves. Follow the well-defined path ahead, ignoring all side turnings, as it winds gently downhill for about ½ mile.

Where a broad track crosses the path (there is a stile opposite) turn right onto the track, a bridleway, and follow it uphill to Angling Spring Farm. In the woodland on the left there is the remains of an ancient chalk-pit and, as the wood is left behind, a large grass field appears. It is here that the walker, if very lucky, may watch the prize bulls of the pedigree Charelais herd being lead-trained by walking with their lead-reins attached to a slow-moving tractor; round and round the field these magnificent beasts are led, heads up and huge haunches rippling. Later on is a field where the calves are kept. Just past the lovely old farmhouse of Angling Spring Farm turn left onto a path leading ahead through Angling Spring Wood. Follow the broad path through the wood ignoring side turnings to emerge into open country on the left and a new conifer plantation on the right. Soon the barns and farm buildings of Andlow's Farm come into view. Walk on past the farm to a road and turn right.

Walk down this road to the main road. Cross with care and enter Broombarn Lane opposite, walking downhill past some comfortable houses set in colourful gardens; the crimsons and golds of leaves on the shrubs in the gardens is eye-catching. Just past the last house on the right is a footpath parallel with the lane which the walker may prefer to take, though the views of tree-bordered hills on the left will be lost behind the high thick hedge. However in the autumn the bold scarlets, crimsons and golds of the dying leaves and the tassles of seeds on the beech trees, hanging like tiny Chinese lanterns, may compensate for this. Where a broad track crosses the footpath, turn left to regain the road and turn right onto it to emerge, after a few yards onto the busy but unclassified road from Great Missenden.

Turn left and cross the road to take a footpath on the right after a few yards. At Coney Cottage leave the main track and take the narrow path ahead on the left winding steeply uphill between hedges and into an open plantation. Here there is a splendid view of the church to the right. Mount a steep bank on the far side of the little plantation, well decked with primroses in the spring, and turn right to walk downhill round the curve of the field edge to a gap in the hedge. Go down the steep bank, sometimes slippery with mud, and follow the path straight across the field to a stile. Over the stile cross the field ahead diagonally toward a railway bridge on the far left. Cross a stile and walk under the bridge, following the path to go over a stile in the far left corner of the field, beside a white house and onto the road. The *Black Horse* public house is a few yards up this road on the right. It is the headquarters of the local Balloon Club and often on summer days, the field behind the pub is bright with colourful monsters lying waiting to be inflated while their owners, beer mug in hand, look skyward for the right moment to go.

Turn right onto the road and, after 150 yards, take the marked path on the left and follow it across the field toward the hedge alongside the main (A413) road. Ignore the stile on the left onto the road and go over the one straight ahead and make for a stile on the right which leads, by a little path, to the car park. To return to the station, cross the car park and turn right into the slip road, cross the High Street at the top and enter Station Road.

Historical notes

Great Missenden: Like many Bucks churches, the church of St Peter & St Paul at Great Missenden stands high on a hill outside the village, overlooking the grounds and buildings of Missenden Abbey. The Abbey was founded in 1133 by William de Missenden and later became the home of a London merchant, James Oldham who, in 1737, built a Venetian-style house on the site.

Prestwood, like many of the local villages, was once famous for its splendid cherry orchards of particularly luscious black cherries, which were harvested and taken to Aylesbury for sale at 2d to 6d a pound. In 1942 it is recorded that the Women's Institute at Prestwood made 1,400 lbs of jam from the cherries.

Flint is widely evident here in the domestic architecture of 17th and 18th century cottages though these are somewhat swamped by new post-war housing.

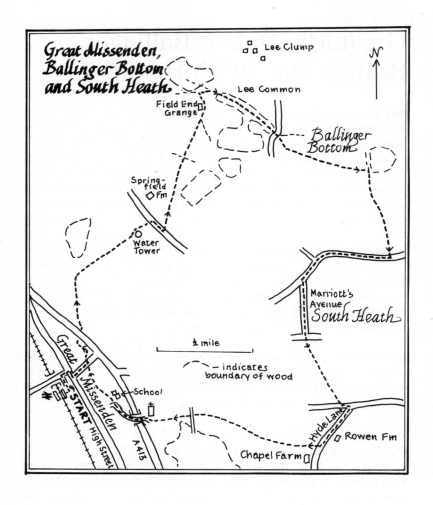

Great Missenden, Ballinger Bottom and South Heath

Introduction: This pretty walk rises steeply over the fields above the Misbourne valley from Great Missenden and then follows a gentle path downhill to Lee Common. Through beechwoods on each side of Ballinger Bottom, the route leads back over fields behind the village of South Heath to Great Missenden. Many Bucks villages have the suffix 'bottom' denoting their positions in the valleys, bounded by high ridges from which there are stupendous views.

Distance: 5 miles – there is some fairly steep climbing but the walk is not demanding, though it is somewhat of a stile-climbing marathon! Some of the walk is on quiet country lanes but the paths through the woods may be muddy after rainfall. OS Landranger Map Sheet 165 Aylesbury & Leighton Buzzard. Pathfinder Sheet SP 80/90 Chesham & Wendover.

Refreshments: There are some excellent pubs in Great Missenden which serve bar meals and snacks. There is nowhere for so much as a cup of tea on the route unless the walker carries it, but there are pleasant spots for a picnic in many places on the way.

How to get there: By train from Marylebone or Baker Street. Please read the Introduction to the book for further train information. By road on the A413 from Amersham. At the second roundabout, 8 miles from Amersham, turn left for Great Missenden. There is a large 'Pay and Display' car park ¼ mile up this road on the right. Join the walk by turning left out of the car park. GR: 894 016

The walk: Turn right out of the station to walk down Station Road to the High Street and cross it to a slip road opposite with the car park on the left and the recreation grounds and village hall on the right. Turn left onto a marked footpath near the end of the road to cross a field. Turn right to cross by a subway under the main road and then go over the stile ahead, ignoring the path coming down hill on the right.

Cross 3 fields diagonally over stiles and, at the third stile, turn right to walk up the field alongside a small brake of woodland to another stile at the top. Pause here to turn round to admire the beautiful spread of landscape down the hill to the deep valley and then up to the tree-fringed hills and fields on the far side. Cross the stile and go over the next field to a wide gap in the hedge opposite and go straight ahead through another gap, making for a tall, white-painted water tower. At the water tower bear left to skirt it and cross the next field, keeping the hedge on the right and the pleasant building of Springfield Farmhouse ahead on the left. Go over a stile at the field end into a lane, turn right and after 200 yards, passing a group of old and delightful cottages on the left, take the path on the left beside a cream-painted house into a field. Bear slightly left to cross it to a stile almost hidden in the high hedge opposite.

Cross the 2 stiles on each side of a grassy track to follow the path ahead. Go over another stile and across a field to yet another stile between a row of conifers and deciduous trees. Go straight ahead across the next field to a gate and stile opposite. Over the stile turn left onto a bridle track and walk down it for ⅓ mile past Field End Grange and a pair of small flint cottages. Just past the cottages turn right at an intersection to walk downhill alongside a beech wood on the left to another stile at the bottom of Lee Common. Turn right to walk across the grassy valley bottom with the houses of Lee Clump high on the hillside to the left. Go over a stile ahead into woods and walk through for about ½ mile to cross another stile onto the lane at Ballinger Bottom. Cross the lane and follow the track opposite, turning right to follow the footpath and bridle-way signs. At a junction keep to the path on the extreme left high above the beeches and alongside the gardens of some pleasant houses. Notice here how holly bushes abound on the wood edge; this is quite a feature of Bucks woodland.

Go over a stile at the wood end into a steeply sloping field; keep to the top of the field following the hedge on the right to a stile almost obscured by holly bushes in the far right corner of the hedge. Cross the stile and follow the path ahead with the varied and ancient hedge now on the left and a large cultivated field on the right. Pheasants can often be seen up here in late summer as they rustle in the hedge or about the field edge for fallen grains of corn. At the far end of the field cross the stile and turn left to go over another stile and turn right into a lane. After a few yards the lane turns sharply right; here keep straight ahead on a narrow path between a high hedge on the right and a broad fenced field on the left. Good blackberries are to be found in the scrubby growth on the fence side! The path emerges into open country at another stile. Cross this and walk straight ahead downhill to a stile on the far side of the field.

The stile leads onto a quiet lane where turn right and walk up it for ½ mile to a road junction; here fork left and continue on toward South Heath, a very prosperous little village on the hill above Great Missenden. After about ⅓ mile turn left into Marriotts Avenue and walk up it between comfortable homes set back in tailored gardens. At the end of the avenue, take the footpath ahead between high hedges and more well-cared-for gardens; there are beehives in a rough, uncultivated bit of field on the right. Cross a little lane and go on along a path and over a stile.

Cross 3 grass fields by stiles to emerge, over the last, on the road from Chesham to Great Missenden. Cross the road into Hyde Lane opposite. Soon, on the left is the beautiful Tudor Rowen Farmhouse with twisted curlicues of chimneys and a magnificent yew-bordered brick path behind the wrought-iron gate. Beside there is a funny little cottage with a grotesquely wavy roof. The huge pile of Chapel Farm lies ahead on the right. About 100 yards past the cottage take the marked path on the right into a small copse and follow it alongside a garden on the left and up a bank into a cultivated field where turn left to walk along the field edge. Go over 2 more stiles to cross 2 cultivated fields; the hedge on the right in the second field is full of huge blackberries in the autumn and is bright with dog rose blossom in early summer. Away to the left is a huge mixed wood, colours heaped up like a rumpled patchwork quilt as the autumn leaves change colour and die. Cross by a gate at the end of the field into a grass field and walk absolutely straight across it to a stile almost at the corner where the tip of the wood dips down. Cross stiles on each side of the narrow Forestry Commission lane and then, bearing slightly left, walk gently downhill toward a thick clump of trees on the right. Go through a kissing gate on the right into the churchyard and follow the path left round the church and left again onto the lane coming up from the village over the A413.

Follow the lane past some pretty cottages on the left to a grass triangle in front of the school. Go round the triangle to take the path on the right running alongside the school into the recreation ground. Cross this by the path alongside it into the slip road on the other side. Turn left to find the car park opposite or to walk up and across the High Street to Station Road.

Historical notes

Great Missenden: Like many Bucks churches, the church of St Peter and St Paul at Great Missenden stands on a hill outside the village, ½ mile or so from its centre. It overlooks the grounds and buildings of Missenden Abbey. The church is a long, low rough-flint structure much 'restored' in 1900 although much of the interior is still of 15th century origin. There are many interesting examples of 17th and 18th century domestic architecture in the High Street.

The Abbey was founded by William de Missenden in 1133 but did not survive the Dissolution of 1534. It later became the home of a London ironmonger, James Oldham, who in 1737 built a Venetian-style house but added neo-Gothic castellated walls and a castellated central pediment. It is now an Adult Education College.

Ballinger & South Heath lie in the hills above Great Missenden; both have now become dormitory suburbs of the nearby towns of

Aylesbury, Amersham and Chesham. The villages were once famous for orchards of particularly luscious cherries which were harvested for jam and the making of a local delicacy, Black Cherry pie. Now only a few old and unproductive trees remain; like the blacksmith and the hedger, they have yielded to a new age and disappeared.

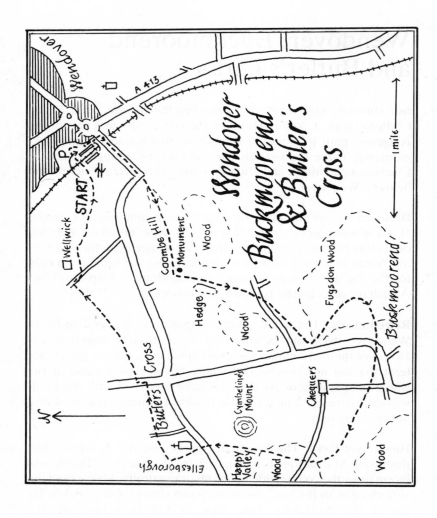

Wendover, Buckmoorend and Butler's Cross

Introduction: This lovely walk reaches the highest point in the Chiltern range, Coombe Hill, and then descends via a part of the Ridgeway path to cross the fields close to Chequers from Buckmoorend. There are beautiful ups and downs through valleys to Ellesborough church and Butler's Cross with a return across the fields to Wendover.

Distance: 8 miles; there is some quite steep climbing up Coombe Hill and some steep downhill work. As these are chalk hills the down bits can be very slippery after rain so need careful negotiating. Some of the stiles are good, some less so and some seem only for the use of long-legged giants! OS Landranger Map Sheet 165 Aylesbury & Leighton Buzzard. Pathfinder Sheet SP 80/90.

Refreshments: There are plenty of places to eat and drink in Wendover itself but nowhere en route to buy refreshments. However there are numerous lovely spots to stop for a picnic, not least the top of Coombe Hill where the sweeping views of the whole of the Vale of Aylesbury can be absorbed with the sandwiches. There are 2 handy cattle troughs to quench the thirst of a hot, panting dog.

How to get there: The 50-minute journey on the Aylesbury line train from Marylebone is a delight in itself; once past Harrow and its environs the countryside opens up dramatically. Please read the Introduction to the book for more information on train times. By car on the A413, the Amersham to Aylesbury road. At the roundabout on entering Wendover, turn left into Pound Street, B4010 and after ¼ mile turn right at the *Shoulder of Mutton* into

69

Station Approach. The 'Pay & Display' car park is just beyond the station. GR: 867 076

The walk: Walk up Station Approach and turn right. Continue walking up the road to a sharp right-hand bend where cross and take the signposted path uphill. At a wooden fence with a 'No Horses' sign on it, take the middle path by means of shallow steps. Very soon, on the left, the path divides, one bit going up steep, rather awkward steps and the other, lower, path winding more gently uphill; take either way as they both join at an open grassy area halfway up the hill. Here there is an excellent prospect of the Vale of Aylesbury with the white buildings of Stoke Mandeville hospital ahead, the chateau-style Rothschild Halton House to the right and the little hamlets of Smokey Row and Clanking away to the left. In summer time the brown meadow and blue chalk butterflies dodge the bumble bees among the dog roses and bramble blossom.

Follow the path to the Monument at the top of the hill, turn left away from it and, keeping a thickset hedge of thorn, gorse and stubby trees on the right, enter a wood after ¼ mile. Follow the well-defined path to a stile; go over it to enter a beech wood and Ridgeway-land, where signs (a yellow arrow surmounted by a white acorn) are visible on the trees. Follow these across a tiny lane to the path opposite. Cross a gravel drive and go straight ahead keeping a look out for the Ridgeway signs, as the path wavers about a bit but is always well-marked. After ¾ mile it swoops sharply to the right and steeply downhill to a cross track. Go across the track and, still following Ridgeway signs, go ahead down the track past Buckmoorend Farm on the left to join a minor road. Although this is a minor road, it is well used so cross with care as there are bends on both sides.

Go over the stile on the far side of the road and follow the obvious path across the field to cross the main drive to Chequers by 2 stiles and into a large field on the other side. There are splendid views of the front elevation of the house and its garden from these fields. At the top of the big field, still keeping to the Ridgeway, turn right to walk along the path with mixed woodland on the left and the side view of Chequers across the field on the right. The orangery, which Mr Edward Heath when Prime Minister made into a swimming pool, can be seen from here.

At the next stile take the path on the right alongside the wood, which in spring is filled with primroses and bluebells, in summer time with purple willow herb and in the autumn with rustling pheasants. The full-leaved summer beech trees afford some grateful shade on a hot sunny day. Over the next stile at the wood end cross a drive, the 'back door' to Chequers, and carry on along a path opposite through a small brake of trees and across a large field with the bald nub of Cymbeline's Mount rising up on the right. Follow the path down steep and uneven steps into the mysterious depths of Happy Valley where the scent of boxwood is quite overwhelming on hot days. Over the stile on the other side pause to look at the huge variety of greens, golds and coppers as the trees fall away into the bottom of the valley. Keep to the chalky little path across the field to a stile and, over it, walk down the field path straight ahead with the majestic pile of Ellesborough church in front; 2 little thatched cottages huddle under its benign wing. Go over the stile at the field end and cross the road to enter the churchyard. Keeping the church on the right and a small brick wall on the left, follow the grassy path downhill by steps to a kissing gate and on to a stile into a field. Cross the field to a makeshift stile in the right corner.

This stile brings you onto a little lane past 2 delightful houses. Cross a farm road after 200 yards and take the marked footpath over fields and stiles to Butler's Cross. Here turn left and cross the road and, after 20 yards or so, take the marked path on the right over a stile. Keep the hedge on the left and then, at a field edge, bear left to keep the fence on the right. Cross the next field absolutely straight to a stile in the hedge into a cultivated field and across it to a high stile into a grassy paddock. Keeping the hedge here closely on the left, walk down to reach the drive of Wellwick House and turn right onto it. As the house is reached notice the tall curlicues of Tudor chimneys and the later, Jacobean, additions to the front elevation. Turn left to walk past the front of the house through the farmyard and, at the far side, turn right along a path across a very big field which has the remains of a stile in the left hand corner close to the start of a hedge. Cross the stile into a grass field and cross it to another one opposite into a large cultivated field with a, usually, well-defined path diagonally across it. The path creeps through the hedge on the far side into the cricket field and over a railway bridge back to the station.

Historical notes

Coombe Hill is said to be the site of an Iron Age fort and the motte and bailey form part of the well-used path to its summit. It is the highest point in the Chiltern range at 830 ft. The monument commemorates the fallen of the Boer War.

Chequers, the country home of successive Prime Ministers, was donated to the nation for this purpose by its owner, Lord Lee of Fareham, in 1922. It lies in the parish of Ellesborough and many Prime Ministers have attended divine service in the church of St Peter and St Paul.

Cymbeline's Mount was the stronghold of the British King Cunobelin or Cymbeline, from whom the villages of Great and Little Kimble derive their names. Relics found there suggest that this was the site of a Romano-British village and a Neolithic hill fort.

Wendover, Aston Hill and Pavis Wood

Introduction: This lovely walk takes in just about everything: a short walk through the attractive little town of Wendover, a climb uphill by ancient, shady woodland paths, spectacular hilltop views, quiet country lanes and a stream. Part of the walk follows the route of the ancient Ridgeway.

Distance: Around 9 miles – make a day's walk of it! There must be time to study the varied landscape and the wealth of wild flowers. OS Landranger Map Sheet 165 Aylesbury & Leighton Buzzard.

Refreshments: You either eat before you go, wait till you get back or take your picnic with you on your back for this walk. Wendover abounds in places of refreshment but, throughout the whole walk, there is no other public house or cafe. However, the Forestry Commission provides delightful picnic areas with benches and tables (and a view thrown in for good measure) in many places and ask only that litter is taken home.

How to get there: By train from Marylebone or Baker Street; please read the Introduction to the book for further information on train services. By road, on the A413 from Amersham toward Aylesbury. At the roundabout at the top of Wendover High Street, turn left onto the B4010 for Princes Risborough and, after a short ¼ mile, turn right into Station Approach alongside the *Shoulder of Mutton*. There is a good 'Pay & Display' car park beyond the station building. GR: 867/076

The walk: Walk up Station Approach and turn left to walk down Wendover High Street. It is wise to cross at the pedestrian crossing

73

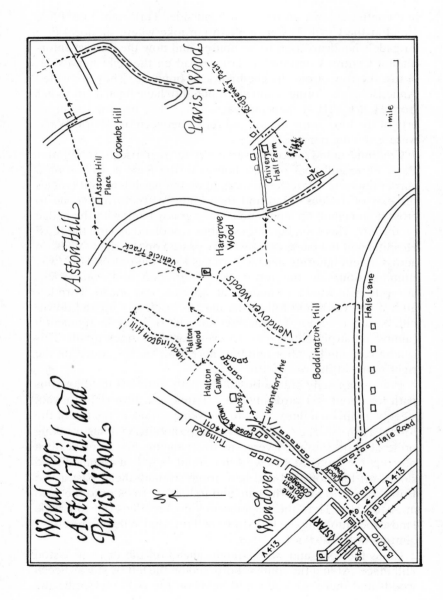

and continue down on the right hand side. Turn right into Tring Road at the Clock Tower, a Victorian joke where the local Fire Brigade's handcart used to be housed and now the Tourist Information Centre. Continue up Tring Road on the right hand side; notice the row of old thatched cottages opposite. They are called Anne Boleyn's Cottages and are reputed to have been a gift to her from Henry VIII at their marriage. Later they became the property of the lord of the manor and rents, between the World Wars, were a shilling per week.

Continue uphill onto the service road as it rises steeply after Bank Farm and goes on past houses to the *Rose & Crown* on a corner opposite. Here continue right on the pavement as it crosses the exit of Tedder Road and then enter Warneford Avenue to cross it and climb up a path on a steep grassy bank with the hedge on the left. This soon becomes scrubby woodland around the RAF Hospital and the backs of houses are passed on the right. Walk on across a field ignoring all side turnings to a stile onto a bridleway running alongside the forest. Here turn left and, very soon, abruptly right where a wooden bar stops the way ahead. Turn left after a few yards and follow the narrow bridleway up and downhill, straight across an intersection and right at a T-junction (almost a hairpin bend) onto an even narrower track uphill. This can be very muddy after rain but there is an 'escape route' on the right to avoid the worst of it.

Emerging finally onto a broad footpath, turn left to follow this path for about 300 yards and, at a T-junction, turn right to walk steeply uphill on a flinty track to the vehicle track at the top of the forest. Turn left and follow the track for about 1½ miles, walking preferably on the grass verge as overhanging tree branches can obstruct the motorist's view. After about ¾ mile a metalled road slopes off left downhill and here forge straight ahead past a 'No Entry' sign. Go round the gate and follow the track onto the road at Aston Hill. Here the magnificent view broadens out to a wide landscape enfolding the little town of Tring and Wilstone reservoir glinting in the distance.

Cross the road and walk straight ahead on the drive to Aston Hill Place. At first the route is bordered on the left by sturdy beech woods and there are cultivated fields on the right. In spring the gorse along this path always seems to be the first to bloom, a cheerful spread of bright yellow; in summer meadow brown and Dingy Skipper butterflies hurry about the purple willow herb and this is the place to look out for deliciously thirst-quenching wild raspberries. At the end of the drive go over a stile to enter the wood and follow the footpath gently downhill. Bold scarlet fly agaric poisonous mushrooms can be found under the trees along the path in the autumn. Notice the splendid view of Ivinghoe Beacon on the left as the wood ends. Wilstone reservoir lies peacefully in the centre of the rolling farmland in the foreground.

Come down onto a lane and turn right; after 50 yards turn left onto a marked footpath beside a house and follow this narrow path over exposed tree-roots and across a large field, keeping the hedge on the left. In summer the field edge is bright with scarlet poppies and yellow ragwort. At the hedge on the far side of the field turn right onto a broader track and follow it to a lane. Notice the bowl-like shape of the landscape formed by the encircling wooded hills ahead. Cross the road intersection and walk straight ahead, following the lane as it curves right past an old cottage with a delightfully uneven and wavy roof. The sweet scent of hedge bedstraw fills the air as great clumps of it flourish on the verge. Where the lane turns right again, keep straight ahead onto a track into Pavis Wood and turn left off the track after a few yards to take a narrower path which climbs steeply uphill. At the top a broader path, the Ridgeway, forms a T-junction and here turn right to follow it along the top of the wood, keeping the wood edge close to the left. Soon the deep hollow of an ancient chalk pit appears on the right.

The path ends in a narrow sunken lane where turn left and, after 10 yards, right over a stile in the field corner, still following the Ridgeway. Walk across the field to a clump of trees to the left and go over the stile there. Follow the path across the next field keeping the hedge on the left to a stile in the far left corner. Creamy-white dog roses and honeysuckle vie with the willow herb to create a dazzling display in the hedge. Go over the stile and turn right onto a fairly busy minor road and walk along it for a short ¼ mile to reach the entrance to Wendover Woods on the left opposite the front entrance of Chivery Hall Farm. Follow the main path, bearing right but diverting neither to left or right for a good mile until the Forestry Commission car park is reached. On the left hand corner of the intersection is a cairn on which is a plaque indicating the winning by the Commission of a Countryside Award for forestry management in 1977. Here turn left along another vehicle track (there are toilets on the right) and walk ahead. Keep a wary eye on traffic on these motor tracks; there is a speed limit but not all drivers observe it.

The path leads past a new plantation of trees on the right among which wild cherry have been planted; their blossom is a cheerful sight in the spring. Also on the right is an excellent picnic area with a grand view over Aylesbury Vale. After about ½ to ¾ mile the track ends in a grassy triangle and here turn left downhill on a broad path for 150 yards and then take the bridle track on the right.

Follow this track down Boddington Hill for about ¾ mile past another 2 tracks merging from the right and down onto a lane. Turn right into the lane and follow it to a T-junction. Cross this busy minor road with care and turn right to take the marked footpath on the left winding downhill to the stream running alongside Sluice Cottage. Go over the little bridge and turn right onto Heron Path, an old ropewalk, and walk along beside the stream. At the junction of the path with Dark Lane, opposite Bucksbridge House, turn left and walk diagonally across the field on the right, called Witchell, to the London Road Service Station. Here turn right and walk up South Street, with some pretty cottages opposite, and left at the roundabout into Pound Street again. Turn right to the station alongside the *Shoulder of Mutton*.

Historical notes

Aston Hill and Boddington Hill both have Iron Age forts on them. On Aston Hill the flat grassy area of the hilltop forms the fort and the deep motte and bailey can be seen on the far side. Boddington's fort is hidden in the woods on the right of the path and here, too, the motte and bailey are clearly discernable.

Aston Hill has another claim to fame in that the young motorcar manufacturer called Martin developed his racing car in nearby

Leighton Buzzard and used Aston Hill to race and test it – hence the Aston Martin.

Wendover: Famous names associated with Wendover are John Hampden and Edmund Burke; both were Parliamentary representatives of Wendover in 1623 and 1796 respectively. The 17th century *Red Lion* in the High Street boasts among its guests the names of Oliver Cromwell, Robert Louis Stevenson and the poet, Rupert Brooke. The infamous 'hanging' Judge Jeffreys lodged at Wellwick House, just outside the town, on his way to the Assizes at Aylesbury.

Wendover, Dunsmore and Kings Ash

Introduction: This walk climbs out of the valley in which Wendover is settled onto a high Chiltern 'ridge' at Dunsmore, along the ridge toward Cobblers Hill and descends over the fields into the valley again. Then there is a climb up the other side of the valley to stupendous views over the rolling countryside and a gentle descent through woodland and along the ancient Ridgeway path back into Wendover.

Distance: A good 8 miles and some fairly steep climbing so allow at least 3 hours with time to admire the views. OS Landranger Map Sheet 165 Aylesbury & Leighton Buzzard. Pathfinder Sheet SP 80/90.

Refreshments: The *Fox* at Dunsmore, which has a pleasant garden, offers bar food. The *Black Horse* has lately become a restaurant. There are pubs and cafes galore in Wendover.

How to get there: By train from Marylebone; please read the Introduction for more information. By road from Amersham on the A413. At the roundabout in Wendover turn left into the B4010 and after a few yards turn right by the *Shoulder of Mutton* into Station Approach where there is a large 'Pay & Display' car park beyond the station building. GR: 867 076

The walk: Walk up Station Approach and turn right. Take a marked path on the left just over the railway bridge and follow it across the field to a lane. Turn right into the lane and then left onto a footpath after 150 yards. Follow the broad path between high beech hedges and then fencing, with splendid horses grazing the

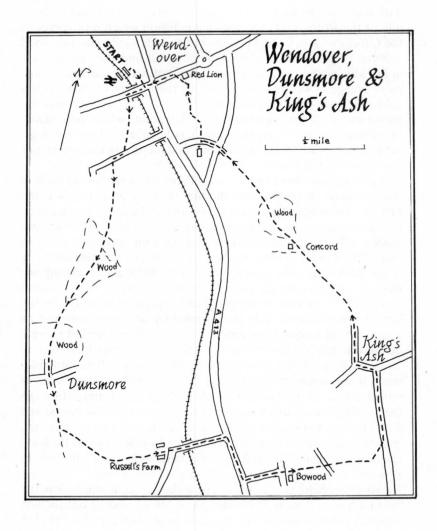

field on the right. Go over 2 stiles and then uphill across a large field to the corner of Coxgrove Wood. Turn round here to see the dark tree-clad outlines of Aston and Boddington Hills and the grey pile of the Rothschild chateau-style mansion which now serves as the Officer's Mess for RAF Halton. Go over a stile into the wood and follow the path bearing right downhill and then right again uphill alongside a wire fence and then left and ahead into Dunsmore village, a sleepy little hamlet on the hilltop. On the left is a field which has been transformed into a play area with a miniature racing-car track and football nets. The pond, which perennially overflowed messily onto the path, has been walled in with logs, planted with water-lilies and willows and a fine mock heron stands guard over the fish in it.

Entering Dunsmore there are pleasant small houses set back in their gardens on the left and the first building on the right is the *Fox* inn. Ignoring all footpath signs, follow the now metalled lane to a crossroads with a duck pond opposite. Cross the road to a track leading to the *Black Horse* and carry on past it for about ¼ mile. There are dog-roses in the summer hedge and distant views of the hills across the valley. When a small house set among the trees is reached take the path on the left through a large wooden gate. Follow the path over a stile and, keeping the hedge on the left, go on down the field past a paddock of fine horses and an abundance of purple foxgloves to the gap, where turn left to walk down the hill through the old stables and farm buildings of Russell's Farm. Pause here to absorb the view of rolling farmland, small farmhouses huddled among the trees and the dark mass of mixed woodland on the right, Cockshoots Wood. Emerge through the farm buildings and follow the lane over the railway bridge and down to the A413. Turn right and cross the road to walk on the grass verge toward Great Missenden for ¼ mile or so to Bowood Lane on the left. Turn left into the lane and, just to the left of Bowood Antiques at the top, take a stile into a field.

Cross this field and 2 stiles over a sunken lane and follow the field path over 2 more fields steeply uphill to emerge onto a lane between a charming white cottage and its kitchen garden. Turn left and follow the lane to Kings Ash. At the T-junction turn left and cross the road and after about 50 yards take a marked bridleway on the right past Robertswood Cottage. There is a pleasanter, usually less muddy, track to follow on the left when the concrete path ends at Concord Farm. The wood, called Robertswood after Sir Robert Barlow, is a Nature Reserve donated by Lady Barlow and now managed by the County Naturalists Trust. Notice the narrow little badger tracks coming out from the path on either side through the undergrowth. Badgers always use the same path on their hunting forays and soon make an obvious and well-worn highway of it. The path narrows at the wood end beside a fenced field and soon creeps downhill through the trees on the right to a broader path and on to the Ridgeway, which follow straight ahead for about 1 mile to a crossroads. In the spring the high banks of this sunken track are covered with huge clumps of purple and white dog violets.

Cross the crossroad into Church Lane and follow it past 2 cottages, a school and the side of the parish church of St Mary the Virgin, 700 years old in 1990. Opposite the lychgate, on the right, is the path alongside Hampden Pond. At the edge of the pond bear left to walk across Hampden Meadow on a made-up path which ends in a lane. Cross to enter the field opposite, the Witchell, walk across it and meet up with the path again on the far side. Very soon bear left again off the path through the edge of a small housing estate and into the coaching-yard of the *Red Lion*. Go through the arch and turn left to walk up the High Street, cross with care at the roundabout into Pound Street and walk up it to the station again.

Historical notes

Wendover: The church of St Mary the Virgin in Wendover is almost a mile from the centre of the village. There is a legend that tells of fairies coming at night to remove the foundations being laid in Witchell and taking them to the site of the present church. After several efforts to build the church in the village the builders gave the evil fairies best and built it where it now stands! Since there has been a church on its site for more than 700 years, this seems a little far-fetched. In 1282 the wooden church was burnt down and the lord of the manor, Roger de Wendover, resolved to build a new one, which was completed in 1290 and still stands today. .

In 1643, during the Civil War, Prince Rupert sent Lord Carnarvon to raid and sack Wendover. Mrs Armitage, the then vicar's wife, baked apple pies to welcome the troops but the Royalists had made off toward Chesham so the pies were eaten by the Parliamentarian troops instead, much to Mrs Armitage's annoyance.

The 17th century *Red Lion* inn has boasted among its guests John Hampden, member of Parliament for Wendover in 1623, Robert Louis Stevenson, Edmund Burke and the poet Rupert Brooke.

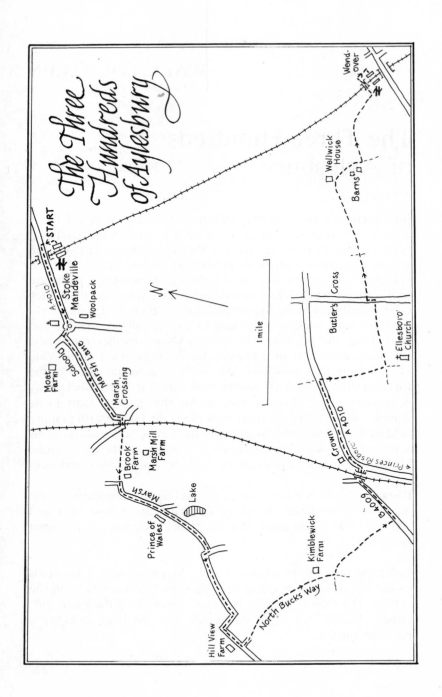

The Three Hundreds of Aylesbury

START

A 4010
Stoke Mandeville
Woolpack
Moat Farm
School
Marsh Lane
Marsh Crossing
Brook Farm
Marsh Mill Farm
Marsh
Prince of Wales
Lake
Hill View Farm
North Bucks Way
Kimblewick Farm
B 4009
← Princes Risboro'
Crown
A 4010
Butler's Cross
Ellesboro' Church
Barns
Wellwick House
Wend-over

N

1 mile

The Three Hundreds of Aylesbury

Introduction: This attractive walk may be one to save for a day after a period of rainfall as much of it is walked on quiet and peaceful country lanes and most of the field paths are grassy. Mud may be encountered on the short bridleway to the hamlet of Marsh and over one or two cultivated fields but most of the paths are well-trodden grassy tracks raised above the level of the fields they cross. Starting at Stoke Mandeville station, on the edge of Metroland, the walk winds along a lane to a small railway crossing and then down the bridleway to Marsh, where another quiet lane meanders drunkenly over the flat, fertile pastureland of the Vale of Aylesbury to Kimblewick. There are spectacular views of the Chiltern slopes ahead. At Kimblewick Farm the North Bucks Way is picked up for about a mile across the fields toward Little Kimble, where there is a short walk along the busy A4010 to more field paths to Butlers Cross and so to the station at Wendover. This is not a round walk but the return to London, or the car at Stoke Mandeville station, can easily be made by train from Wendover.

Distance: 7½ to 8 miles – an easy, level and undemanding walk, much of it on lanes. Some of the stiles are rather high and awkward. OS Landranger Map Sheet 165 Aylesbury & Leighton Buzzard.

Refreshments: The *Woolpack* at Stoke Mandeville lies a few yards to the left at the crossroads and the *Crown* at Kimble is on the A4010. The *Prince of Wales* is about ½ way along the route, just outside Marsh. All serve bar meals and the *Woolpack* has a pleasant garden.

How to get there: By train from Marylebone or Baker Street; please read the Introduction to the book for further train information. By car on the A413, Amersham to Aylesbury. Two and a half miles on the Aylesbury side of Wendover, at a roundabout, turn left onto the A4010 signposted for Princes Risborough and park the car in the 'Pay & Display' car park at Stoke Mandeville station ¼ mile up the road on the left. GR: 829 106

The walk: On leaving the station turn left and cross the railway by a bridge, walking on the pavement for ½ mile to a large road junction with a roundabout. Here cross the road ahead to enter a small lane opposite on the left signposted 'Marsh and Bishop-stone'. The old 19th century brick and flint schoolhouse lies on the right and, very shortly on the right, is the entrance to Moat Farm, once the property of John Hampden. On the left the flat pasture-land of the Vale meets the high ridge of the Chiltern hills; Coombe Hill, the highest point in the range, stands out with its obelisk-like Monument on the top. After ¾ mile Marsh Crossing is reached; here turn right over the railway into the lane as for Bishopstone and, after 20 yards, take the marked bridleway on the left. Walk ahead, ignoring side turnings, for a short ½ mile to a lane. Here turn left to walk past Marsh Mill Farm and Brook Farm and through the hamlet of Marsh. Follow the lane ahead and soon the *Prince of Wales* pub appears on the right. During the summer a group of garden tables and chairs stands on the grassy verge opposite.

Carry on past the front of the *Prince of Wales*; on the left, surrounded by a clump of rather scrubby trees, is a pleasant small lake. Bear right and then left as the road curves past a funny little brick tower and keep on along the lane, winding again right and then left, until Hill View Farm is reached on the right. Here there is a strange looking tall, brick house with a Dutch-style mansard roof. Opposite the house turn off the lane to the left along a track marked 'North Bucks Way'; ahead are splendid views of Pulpit Hill, its bare horseshoe-shaped slope surrounded by trees, the bald crown of Cymbeline's Mount and a first glimpse of Ellesborough church standing high on its own little hillock. Skirt a new barn conversion on the left and follow the track ahead over the fields with wide open countryside all around. Go over stiles and a small footbridge to follow the path, over more stiles, to Kimblewick Farm lying back on the left. Go over a stile in the fence on the left to walk straight across the next field and over stiles to turn right onto the metalled drive to the farm.

Walk up the drive for a few yards to a lane and cross to take the footpath marked opposite. Turn right and walk down the side of the field to a road, the B4009. There is a newly-opened pub just a few yards up the road on the right but, if you are not seeking refreshment, turn left here and follow the road downhill gently for ¼ mile to walk through a bridge under the railway and out onto the A4010, which can be quite a busy road. Turn left here and walk on the pavement (the *Crown* is a few yards along on the left) for about ¾ mile, when the pavement ends abruptly at a bus stop. Now you must cross the road to continue on the pavement on the right for a few yards. Against the hedge on the left is a sign marking footpaths in both directions; here go over, or round, a stile on the right obscured in the thickset hedge and go straight ahead alongside a garden on the left and then beside a slight rise in the ground. Go through the gap in the hedge and bear a little right past a muddy pond surrounded by scrubby thorn bushes to a stile in the right corner into a thicket. Across the fields are closer views of Cymbeline's Mount and the lovely tower of Ellesborough church. To the left is Coombe Hill.

Walk through the wood over a tiny tumbling stream and a stile on the far side and on across the next field to a stile and gate in the left corner. Go over the stile and turn left into a metalled track past a pretty cottage and a larger, white-painted house in an immaculate garden with some interesting topiary. Go ahead along a grassy field path, ignoring the turning coming in on the right, and follow the path over 3 fields and their accompanying stiles to emerge onto the road at Butlers Cross. Turn left here and walk down for 20 yards then take the field path on the right, just past the colourful little Southfield Nursery. Follow the path ahead and, where the fence appears to cut it in half, keep left, leaving the fence on the right, to a stile at the top of the field. Cross 3 fields straight ahead over stiles; the middle, cultivated one, has some-times a rather obscure path but it is straight ahead to the stile opposite. At the end of a grass field, part orchard, turn right to walk down the drive of Wellwick House. Notice the charming curlicues on the 16th century chimneys and the Jacobean front elevation of this lovely old house where 'hanging' Judge Jeffreys lodged when he visited Aylesbury Assizes. Below is a delightful hotch-potch of timber-framed barns. Turn left at the farmyard to walk up between the barns and a huge Dutch barn where the hay is stored; the sweet scent of it is pervasive on a hot afternoon. Just beyond the hay barn turn right into a big field and walk across it on a raised grassy path, in the autumn bordered with toadflax and scabious, to a point where a hedge comes down to meet it. Here go over a rather makeshift stile and turn left to walk across the meadow to the stile opposite. The fence on the left was supported, until a few years ago, by tall, sturdy elms all of which were felled when Dutch elm disease overtook them. The rabbits haven't noticed and dozens of them still inhabit the intricate maze of warrens among the roots.

Cross the stile into a large cultivated field and walk diagonally across it on a well-trodden path to the hedge opposite. Creep through the hedge into the cricket field and walk across it and the footbridge to arrive at Wendover station.

Historical notes

Moat Farm, Stoke Mandeville, is an L-shaped 16th century farmhouse, once the property of John Hampden, Member of Parliament for Wendover in 1623. It was the tax, 'Ship Money', on this property that he refused to pay, riding into Great Kimble church on horseback and disrupting Morning Prayer to demand of his tenants that they follow his example.

Cymbeline's Mount was the fortress of the British king, Cunobelin, from whom the two villages of Great and Little Kimble derive their names. There is also a Neolithic hill-camp nearby.

Ellesborough church, the church of St Peter & St Paul, is of flint with a tall embattled tower in mixed Perpendicular and Decorated styles. The church was much restored and 'Victorianised' between 1854 and 1871. It is to this church that many Prime Ministers come from nearby Chequers for Sunday worship.

Beaconsfield, Penn and Forty Green

Introduction: Although not strictly in Metroland, Beaconsfield is easily accessible by train from Marylebone and is an ideal starting point for walking. Like Amersham, Beaconsfield is divided into an old and a new town, the former being a charming, historic old town on the A40, the old route from London to the South Midlands and Wales. The new town sprang up with the coming of the railway in 1862 and has some places of interest but it is mostly a very up-market dormitory for wealthy commuters. This very scenic walk up to the historic village of Penn, 550 ft above sea level, and back over fields and through beechwoods, starts and ends along the network of small footpaths which weave their way around the back of the town behind the spacious gardens of the comfortable houses of Beaconsfield. Penn village is explored and the return takes the walker into the hamlet of Forty Green, where not even a village shop now remains to serve the local needs.

Distance: 7 miles – the climbing is quite gentle, as is the scenery, and this deserves time to appreciate. If the walker is fortunate enough to find Penn's Holy Trinity church open, a look at this is well worth a few moment's extra time so allow a good 3 hours. OS Landranger Map Sheet 175 Reading & Windsor. Pathfinder Sheet SU 89/99.

Refreshments: About halfway along the walk is the *Crown* at Penn which sits on the hilltop with superb scenery dropping downhill behind it. It has a pleasant garden area and serves bar meals and snacks. Beaconsfield Old Town abounds with eateries and pubs, the most famous of which is the *Saracen's Head*. In the new town

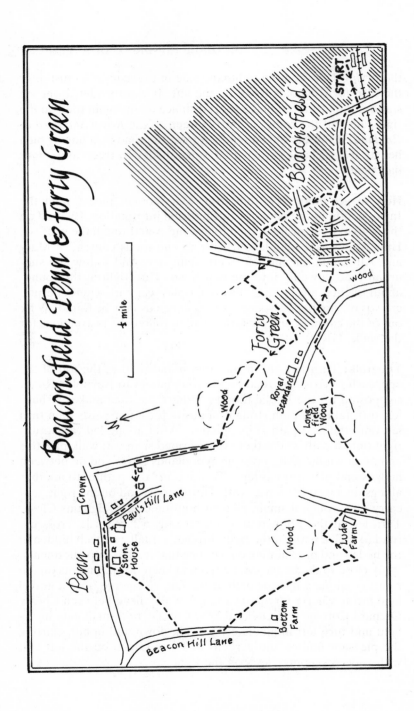

Beaconsfield, Penn & Forty Green

START

Beaconsfield

Wood

Forty Green

Royal Standard

Long field Wood

Wood

Lude Farm

Crown

Penn

Paul's Hill Lane

Stone House

Wood

Bottom Farm

Beacon Hill Lane

N

¼ mile

the *Frying Pan* is on the righthand side of the main road just after the turn for Reynolds Road on the left. If you turn left from the station, the *Coffee Shop* is a short distance up the main road on the right. Just off the route, at Forty Green, is the *Royal Standard of England*, 900 years old and hidden from the road by a hugely high hedge. It has a large garden area, some shaded by trees, and serves bar meals.

How to get there: By train from Marylebone; please read the Introduction to the book for further train information. By road on the M40 to Beaconsfield, then follow the A40 through the wide old High Street to a roundabout with an enormous church, St Mary and All Saints, on the left. Turn right here and follow the suburban road downhill into the new town. Turn right at the roundabout to enter a very large 'Pay & Display' car park where, despite crowds of shoppers, a space for the car can usually be found. Walk out of the car park and cross the road to follow the instructions for the walk. GR: 941 912

The walk: Turn left out of the station and right at the top of the approach to cross the road by the roundabout to Reynolds Road, signposted for the Public Library. Where the road makes a sharp left turn take the path straight opposite for a few yards then turn left onto the next path at its junction. After about 250 yards, turn right onto a path where there is a 3-armed signpost; walk past this and on down the path, crossing Woodlands Drive and on between hedges and pleasant gardens. Turn left off this path onto another alongside a wooden fence, with Throshers Wood on the right, and carry on through a small, elegant housing estate, Eghams Close. Turn left at the T-junction and after only a few yards, cross the road to take a path on the right through a small gate well hidden in the hedge and proclaiming on a notice that it leads into allotments. Walk close to the hedge on the left and keep the allotments on the right; go along a narrow path at the end to emerge onto a gravel lane facing Cherry Orchard Cottage. Walk ahead between Cherry Orchard Cottage and Orchard Way Cottage to a small gate into a field and turn left immediately to walk down and uphill, skirting the pleasant houses and gardens of Forty Green on the left and with wide, sweeping views on the right.

At the end of the hedge go over a stile and across a little field to another, bearing slightly right toward Saunders Wood. Enter the wood over a stile and keep to the lefthand path along the wood edge. Follow this well-trodden path through the wood and alongside a hedge for about ½ mile when the country will open up on the left by some farm buildings and the track, now a metalled driveway, will continue alongside the wood on the right. Follow the drive for a good ¼ mile and, just past a large red brick house away to the left, turn left onto a path which crosses the field and enters Pauls Hill Lane through a little thicket at the end.

Turn right onto the lane and walk up past some charming 17th–18th century cottages of flint and brick on the right and the splendid pile of The Knoll on the left. At the top of the lane is a grassy triangle on which stands a whitened and gnarled hollow tree trunk and opposite this is the *Crown* with a beautiful vista of wooded countryside rolling down behind it. Holy Trinity church lies on the left. Here turn left and cross the road to the pavement and walk past the church and some handsome buildings and houses. Just past Stone House, on the left, cross the road again to follow the bridletrack by Groves Barn and Oakmead House. Keep on gently downhill on the flinty track to a Y-junction where bear right over a ditch and, after about 10 yards, go over a stile on the left to enter a rough, uncultivated field. Follow the narrow path uphill past a large single oak tree. Go over the stile by the hedge on the far side and turn right at the end of the path through a small group of houses to Beacon Hill Lane.

Turn left onto the lane and walk down between pleasant houses for about ¼ mile. Go over a stile on the left onto a marked footpath and follow this over the next stile onto a track opposite, soon passing a large vineyard on the right. A pretty little farm of warm red brick lies in the hollow to the right. At the end of the vineyard go over a stile on the left and across a field to a gate. Go over another stile on the left to walk across the field behind Lude Farm toward a wood. At the edge of the wood take the stile on the right to walk down the field with Lude Farm on the right, to a stile on the far side onto a tiny lane. Turn right onto the lane and, after 20 yards, take the marked path on the left over a stile/gate. Go over another stile and turn right onto a track going downhill. After a few yards turn left alongside a hedge to walk down a grass field to a stile in the valley bottom. Go over the stile and straight ahead uphill across a cultivated field (the path is usually reinstated after ploughing) to a wood. Enter the wood by a stile and follow the narrow path through a scrubby and stunted copse to a fine beech-wood where, ignoring the stile on the left, bear right into a large field and follow the path down and uphill to go over a stile to the left of a double-pole electricity pylon.

Walk ahead through an old and now rather unproductive orchard to a stile in the hedge at the right hand corner. Cross this and go down a little bank onto a narrow lane. If you wish to visit the *Royal Standard of England*, which has quite a history as well as a reputation for hospitality, turn left here and walk up the lane for 200 yards. The pub is on the right by a little triangle of grass and hidden by a tall hedge. It is an interesting building with many unusual features including a large iron grille over the lock on the front door. If you are not for turning off the route, turn right into the lane at the stile and walk gently uphill, past the little lane coming in on the right, for about 300 yards to a telephone kiosk on the right. Here take the path on the right over a gigantic stile and across a lovely curving field, making for Hogback Wood. Follow the path straight ahead through the wood and over the stile at the top, ignoring the one on the left. Walk along the path ahead between high garden fences and crossing 3 residential roads to paths on the far side. At the next road turn right and then cross the road at the sign, turn right again at the end of a cul-de-sac and left at the next footpath sign. This path leads directly back to the 3-armed signpost noted on the outward route so here turn right/left to follow the original path back into Beaconsfield, remembering to turn right after 250 yards to follow the straight path back to Reynolds Road.

Historical notes

Beaconsfield, the name means 'field in the beeches', is still sur-rounded by beechwoods lying on gently sloping chalk hills. The old town lies about a mile to the south of the station at the end of a pleasant suburban road. The new town arose around the railway station and is mainly of large comfortable houses in spacious gardens but, much earlier on, Edmund Burke, Member of Parliament for Wendover bought his house, Gregories, in 1768 and here gave hospitality to famous artists and writers of his time, among them Crabbe, Sheridan, Garrick and Johnson. The original house was burned down in 1813. G.K. Chesterton wrote his 'Father Brown' stories when he lived at Overroads in Grove Road.

Close to the car park, in Warwick Road is Bekonscot, which was started by a model railway enthusiast in the early 1930s. Around the circuit of railway in his garden he began to make and stage models of 'village' houses, cottages and shops and, of course, a church. The area and the models have grown and grown since the early days and working models now include an airport, docks, a fun-fair and 2,500 ft of railway with 5 stations.

Penn: William Penn of Pennsylvania was distantly related to the family who owned Penn Manor. He was proud of his village connection and 4 of his grandsons are buried in the churchyard. The church of Holy Trinity is of Saxon origin, has a tall roughcast flint tower and nave and a brick chancel. It is said that the view from the church tower is the widest in England; 5 counties can be seen. Around 1380 the church roof was raised and supported by 10 carved corbels. The black tie-beams and traceried arches contrast strikingly with the bare, whitewashed walls on which hang 2 funeral hatchments, an early Queen Anne coat of arms and a Lord's Prayer of the early 19th century. The box pews and the pulpit with spiral stair-rails are 18th century; the latter was brought from Curzon Street, Mayfair chapel in 1899.

The Penn family owned the manor and the adjoining Beaumond Manor, from the 13th century until 1731 when, on the death of Roger Penn, the County Sheriff, it passed to the Curzons and thence to the present Earl Howe. The Knoll is a 17th century house in warm red brick with a heavily moulded cornice. It is one of many such delightful old houses seen along the village street in their neat little gardens.

The twin villages of Penn and Tylers Green were once the centre of a flourishing tiling industry and, in the 14th century, one man, Simon the Pavyer, developed the technique of burning glazed floor tiles in 2 colours. The tiles became so famous that they were used at Westminster and Hampton Court Palaces and at Windsor Castle.

Forty Green is a small neat hamlet, a suburb of its grander neighbour, Beaconsfield, but its claim to fame and its pride is its pub, the one and only one so-named, the *Royal Standard of England*. During the Civil War, when there were skirmishes in and among the beechwoods between Roundhead and Royalist troops, the inn became the Royalist HQ and was dubbed 'The Standard' by the soldiers. It is said that Charles I took refuge there and, at the Restoration of the Monarchy in 1660, Charles II gave his consent to the re-naming of the inn with a 'Royal' in front!